Integral Christianity
The Way of Embodied Love

Integral Christianity: The Way of Embodied Love

ISBN: 978-1-7350112-3-3

Published by Bright Alliance

First Edition

Printed and Bound in the United States of America

Layout and design by Brad Reynolds: integralartandstudies.com
Cover cross: Nancy Rebal for *San Damiano Crucifix*, St. Francis of
Assisi Catholic Church, Frisco, TX, USA
Cover design: Tri Widyatmaka

For more information on Rollie Stanich see:
wayembodiedlove.com

Integral Christianity
The Way of Embodied Love

Roland Michael Stanich

BRIGHT
ALLIANCE

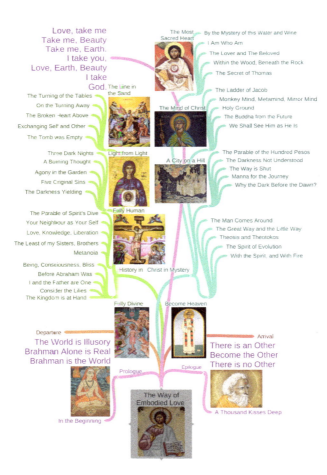

Love, take me
Take me, Beauty
Take me, Earth.
I take you,
Love, Earth, Beauty
I take
God.

The Most Sacred Heart

By the Mystery of this Water and Wine
I Am Who Am
The Lover and The Beloved
Within the Wood, Beneath the Rock
The Secret of Thomas

The Line in the Sand

The Turning of the Tables
On the Turning Away
The Broken Heart Above
Exchanging Self and Other
The Tomb was Empty

The Mind of Christ

The Ladder of Jacob
Monkey Mind, Metamind, Mirror Mind
Holy Ground
The Buddha from the Future
We Shall See Him as He Is

Three Dark Nights
A Burning Thought
Agony in the Garden
Five Original Sins
The Darkness Yielding

Light from Light

A City on a Hill

The Parable of the Hundred Pesos
The Darkness Not Understood
The Way is Shut
Manna for the Journey
Why the Dark Before the Dawn?

The Parable of Spirit's Dive
Your Neighbour as Your Self
Love, Knowledge, Liberation
The Least of my Sisters, Brothers
Metanoia

Fully Human

The Man Comes Around
The Great Way and the Little Way
Theosis and Theotokos
The Spirit of Evolution
With the Spirit, and With Fire

Being, Consciousness, Bliss
Before Abraham Was
I and the Father are One
Consider the Lilies
The Kingdom is at Hand

History in Christ in Mystery

Fully Divine

Become Heaven

Departure
The World is Illusory
Brahman Alone is Real
Brahman is the World

Arrival
There is an Other
Become the Other
There is no Other

Prologue

Epilogue

The Way of Embodied Love

In the Beginning

A Thousand Kisses Deep

Table of Contents

Dedication

FOR ROBERT STANICH
Born at Spirit River, AB, Canada January 3, 1935
Died at Calgary, AB, Canada June 21, 2020

the gentlest hand I've ever held
the broadest shoulder, strongest arm
that lifted countless bales of hay
that lost a thumb up on the farm
have traced their way to great release
to where the Spirit meets the Peace

the New Year's Boy in '35
out of St. Peter and St. Paul
the last of Grandma's *boysiches*
from living waters flowed his call
with every breath, till breathing cease
out where the Spirit meets the Peace

the strappin' farmboy found his love
who gave her hand the day he knelt
and Rappin' Robert always said
"you play the hand that you've been dealt"
you played so well, to such increase
at last the Spirit meets the Peace

we longed for you all through the fall
you kept a vigil in your room
and willed to love us one last week
before you turned toward the tomb
where love will rest, yet not decrease
from where the Spirit meets the Peace

on Father's Day you slipped away
back to St. Peter and St. Paul
back to the country way up North
and still you smile upon as all
so *laku noć*, Dad, sweet release
up where the Spirit meets the Peace

FOREWORD

KEN WILBER

Think about our earliest tribal ancestors. Did they possess atoms, molecules, cells, organisms? Surely they did. But were they aware of them? Did atoms or molecules or cells enter their awareness at all? Surely they did not. Those items were not discovered until over a hundred years ago. So I'd like to distinguish between those two facts. I'd like to refer to when those atoms, molecules, and cells entered a human being's awareness—and I'll call that ex-istence (or standing out in awareness, existing in awareness)—and I'll distinguish that from when those items simply were part of an overall reality whether humans were aware of them or not—which I'll call sub-sistence. So for our ancestors, atoms, molecules, and cells already fully sub-sisted in reality, but they had not yet come into any sort of ex-istence in a human being's awareness.

I want to make this distinction because recent research into the minds of human beings has discovered items that are clearly important for us to know about, but if we only learned about these items in the last few years, does this mean that our ancestors—of, say, one or two thousand years ago—could not have been aware of them? In other words, what if these new discoveries had sub-sisted in human beings for thousands of years, but were discovered, or came into ex-istence for human awareness, only a year or two ago?

What if these new discoveries deal with significant areas such as the stages of human development that lead to important areas of awareness, areas that are instrumental in, say, something like a traditional experience of Enlightenment or Awakening? And that by following these newly discovered stages, humans could indeed reach a traditional Enlightenment with much greater speed and certainty? Would this mean that the traditional approaches to Enlightenment, followed by people several thousand years ago, would not have access to these newly discovered stages? If not, what is the reality of these stages—are they really there, or did they simply come into being when they were first discovered?

It turns out that researchers are actually faced with these types of discoveries—and questions. New theories of human consciousness and its development have indeed uncovered several major areas—that include several stages of development that human awareness and consciousness undergoes—and these areas are directly related to traditional areas of Enlightenment or Awakening. One of the better known of these new theories is called Integral Theory ("Integral" because it claims to be more inclusive and comprehensive). Among many other things, Integral Theory is a fairly comprehensive look at the overall stages of development through which consciousness travels in its total growth and evolution, including those that relate directly to Enlightenment or Awakening. And so the question becomes, if this is so, then did the original people who were practicing a particular type of Enlightenment exercise (Christian, Hindu, Buddhist, Arabic, Jewish)—could they have been using these newly discovered stages in their own practice? And further, could someone today undertake the same traditional practices, but now add the newly discovered stages of development to help them reach their own Enlightenment more rapidly and more surely?

The answer seems to be a strong "yes." What we need to understand here is that, to the extent these newly discovered stages are real, then they sub-sisted even in the original practitioners of the particular tradition (although they did not ex-ist in their aware-ness). And what is happening now is that practitioners are bringing these stages into ex-istence, they are mak-ing them a conscious part of their being. Just as the original traditional practitioners were not likely to be aware of atoms, molecules, or cells, neither were they directly aware of these newly discovered stages of de-velopment. But in the same sense, just as virtually any practitioner today can become aware of the ex-istence of atoms, molecules, and cells, so any practitioner to-day can become aware of the ex-istence of these newly discovered stages of development, and they can then simply translate their original practice using these new stages.

And that is one of the things that Integral Theory helps people to do. Of course, Integral Theory can be used in all sorts of areas besides spiritual practice. But I'm focusing on spiritual practice because that is what this book is about—namely, the spiritual practice of Jesus Christ. What this book does is take several differ-ent areas from Integral Theory and then translate a tra-ditional Christian practice using these new additions. These areas include ones that are called Waking Up, Growing Up, Clearing Up, and Showing Up. Each of those areas include the results of recent research into human growth and development, adding items such as stages, states, and shadow elements—elements not generally found in the traditional practice of Christianity, but ones that can be easily translated so as to apply to all of them. And that is what Rollie does in this book. He takes areas of human development that sub-sist in all humans, and helps us to readily turn them into areas that ex-ist in each of us, so that we can use the research findings of Integral Theory to help us accelerate our spiritual practice. (And believe me, it's a lot more interesting than this rather dull explanation!)

So welcome to a genuine practice of an Integral Christianity. It will help you to more readily move through the states of Waking Up (which are similar to the traditional Enlightenment or Awakening experiences), and help you evolve and develop through the stages of Growing Up (which are newly-discovered stages of development that all people move through), and help you to Clean Up (or re-integrate various unconscious shadow elements), and Show Up (or include such items as the Good, the True, and the Beautiful)—thus bringing a truly comprehensive or Integral approach to your spirituality. This more comprehensive approach takes all of those areas that sub-sist in all people and helps them to consciously ex-ist, so that you will pass through all of those areas in a conscious and aware fashion, and not in an unconscious and haphazard fashion. Because what Integral Theory has discovered is that all people possess all of those areas—they sub-sist in everybody—and so you can either consciously embrace their ex-istence or stumble through their sub-sistence in an unknowing and unconscious fashion. It is probably clear that it is much better to consciously, holistically, and comprehensively embrace all of them in ex-istence, not stumble through them all in sub-sistence—and that is what an Integral Christianity will allow you to do. Further, this understanding will help you integrate not just Christianity but any spirituality, or indeed simply your overall life in general. In this book, Rollie will act as a guide to just that process of discovering a more Integral approach.

I'm delighted to introduce this approach to you, and I hope that it will indeed help you to more readily and surely discover your own Christ Consciousness.

Integral Christianity
The Way of Embodied Love

PROLOGUE

In the beginning was the Word, and the Word was with God, and the Word was God. ²He was in the beginning with God. ³All things came into being through him, and without him not one thing came into being. ⁴What has come into being in him was life, and the life was the light of all people. ⁵The light shines in the darkness, and the darkness did not overcome it.

⁶There was a man sent from God, whose name was John. ⁷He came as a witness to testify to the light, so that all might believe through him. ⁸He himself was not the light, but he came to testify to the light. ⁹The true light, which enlightens everyone, was coming into the world.

¹⁰He was in the world, and the world came into being through him; yet the world did not know him. ¹¹He came to what was his own, and his own people did not accept him. ¹²But to all who received him,

who believed in his name, he gave power to become [13]children of God, who were born, not of blood or of the will of the flesh or of the will of man, but of God.

[14]And the Word became flesh and lived among us, and we have seen his glory, the glory as of a father's only son, full of grace and truth. (John 1: 1–14)

> *The world is illusory;*
> *Brahman alone is real;*
> *Brahman is the world.*

> —Adi Shankara

DEPARTURE

There are two teachers who have influenced my spiritual path in particularly deep ways and in retrospect, it's clear to see why. I met Father Thomas Keating, giant among Christian contemplatives, in my 20's, at a time when I was bursting into rational thought, questioning most of what I'd been taught, and deeply curious about the awakening and enlightenment pointed out by the Great Ways of the East. Father Thomas's simple presence transmitted that awakening and enlightenment, though he would never claim such a thing. In him I knew someone who had found what I was looking for, in the distance along the very path I was walking on! In Boulding's First Law, "if something exists, then it must be possible." So my soul found rest, and the form of my Bodhisattva vow became not to remain on this side of Nirvana but rather, to remain on my path, knowing that one billion Catholics and two billion Christians were also on that path, and that we could all draw from the realization of Father Thomas, who said to be a saint was a good start, but that the voice of the calling rang deeper: to become "no thing."

I encountered the second teacher at the edge of my pluralistic stage, looking for something deeper than "all religions are saying the same thing" and trying to find an approach that would have some traction in the world, which by all accounts was going to hell. And after a 10-day silent retreat with Father Thomas I had a two-hour meeting with Ken Wilber (on what was the strangest day of my life—but that's a story for another book). Wilber could move me into a nondual state within moments, simply by pointing it out, and would then say to me—no longer I but now *I-I*—"fill this place with you." But he showed me, too, that however high the vista from which I looked out, it was paramount to open the widest possible aperture to take the most panoramic picture I could, so as to lose the least possible in translation.

In retrospect, these teachers gave me *states* and *stages*, at critical junctions in my life, averting what might have been the turning away, in my case. A prophet is not one who sees the future but rather, one who sees clearly the signs of the times. And these two saw the signs of my time, with abundant clarity.

Father Thomas continued to deepen in his teaching and practice; Wilber continued to iterate and clarify his thought, finding the simplicity beyond the complexity and articulating a model with the minimum elements necessary to get a Kosmos going, but no more—and no fewer—than that. My two teachers were great friends, and Father Thomas thanked Ken for "giving us the words, the vocabulary, with which to discuss the Mystery." Their thought is potent together: consider Father Thomas's "become no thing" together with Wilber's "when I am not an object, I am God."

Wilber taught that human development can be seen from the inside (*states*) and the outside (*stages*) and although there is some relationship between the two, they are best seen as distinct journeys, both of which every human being embarks upon, knowingly or not. The journey through states is taken unconsciously by each of us every day and every night, through waking, dreaming, and deep sleep. The world's religious traditions have known this for ages and sought to extend our *wakefulness* through all these great states. By contrast, the journey through stages was only understood by modernity, which is concerned with relative truth, and involves a hidden map through which we all move, though we seldom do so consciously and intentionally. Crucially, what we experience in our *state* is unpacked and interpreted through our *stage*. And crucially, as we advance along our twin journeys of states and stages, parts of us can fail to make the jumps when the rest of us are ready, and split off into *shadow*. We are all stained-glass windows, and at all of our feet there are colorful shards of our selves scattered across the chapel floor. Nonetheless, we're all mean to be a masterpiece, and in truth, we all Always Already are.

Wilber distilled his AQAL Model and its implications for our lives into an injunction for everyone, breathtaking in its simplicity:

WAKE UP

GROW UP

CLEAN UP

SHOW UP

This means—once you know what Integral reveals from the simplicity beyond complexity—it becomes incumbent on you to cultivate your states of consciousness (WAKE UP), your stages of consciousness (GROW UP), to tend to the split-off selves which inadvertently didn't make the developmental jumps (CLEAN UP), and to live every day to deepen evolution in the intentional, behavioral, cultural and social aspects of your life (SHOW UP). In other words: to experience body, mind, and spirit in self, culture, and nature. Or to look within your "I," and look within our "we," and look outside of your "I," and outside of our "we," and from the deepest Awareness you can cultivate, move decisively in every NOW—the only moment we will ever have—so that it can be embraced by the next moment as more good, more true and more beautiful.

In these chapters I look at the injunction to WAKE UP / GROW UP / CLEAN UP / SHOW UP as it was followed by Jesus of Nazareth, *Christ in History*. Though we want to avoid the raucous scene that took place in *Dead Poet's Society*—Mr. Keating exhorting his literature class to rip out the textbook pages on mathematically determining a poem's value—looking at how Jesus followed this fourfold injunction can prove abundantly fruitful for our own journeys. Jesus taught us to follow him: this involves a profound emptying and learning from him by *meta-noia*—changing our minds.

Next, I examine the same injunction as undertaken by *Christ in Mystery*. Consider the extent that Immanuel Kant's categorical imperative applies:

> Act only according to that maxim whereby you can, at the same time, will that it should become a universal law.

Jesus (*Christ in History*) certainly acted in this way. That is only half the story; the question is, how does the categorical imperative apply to *Christ in Mystery*? What does WAKE UP / GROW UP / CLEAN UP / SHOW UP mean now, in retrospect of Jesus' taking up the injunction? We know what Jesus *would* do; the question is, what *will* Christ do?

So we embark upon our journey into Integral Christianity, in the tradition of David Steindl-Rast, Cynthia Bourgeault, Richard Rohr, Elaine Pagels, Jim Marion, Ilia Delio, Paul Smith, Nan C. Merril, David Frenette, and others, with the auspicious retinue of Thomas Keating, Joseph Boyle, Wayne Teasdale, Bernadette Roberts, Bruno Barnhart, Beatrice Bruteau and Raimon Panikkar blessing us from beyond. With all respect to the Four Noble Truths of old, we have four noble truths anew: wake up, grow up, clean up, show up. We have them lived definitively by *Christ in History*. And we have *Christ in Mystery*, who will do "greater things than these," since Jesus was going to the Father, in order to send the Spirit....

Rollie Stanich
Ascension Thursday
May 13, 2021
Vancouver, B.C., Canada

PART I

Christ In History

ONE
FULLY DIVINE

In my beginning is my end.

Twenty centuries ago, a man rose from the waters of the river Jordan, having been baptized by the itinerant Jewish preacher named John the Forerunner. John had been preaching in the wilderness of Judea and saying, "Repent (literally, *metanoia,* make a transformative change of heart), for the kingdom of heaven has come near." When the people wondered in their hearts whether he could be the promised Messiah, he answered them all:

> I baptize you with water. But one who is more powerful than I will come, the straps of whose sandals I am not worthy to untie. He will baptize you with the Holy Spirit and fire. (Luke 3:16)

As Jesus of Nazareth emerged in prayer, John saw

the Spirit "descend and remain" on him, and a voice was heard: "You are my son, the beloved; with you I am well pleased." Jesus followed the first of Ken Wilber's four new noble truths: WAKE UP. The ripples from his arising still lap gently on our shores, two millennia later, with the good news of how a life lived as love without limits can transform the world.

Being, Consciousness, Bliss

Though we are two millennia in the wake of Jesus, in some sense we are closer than ever to Christ. Modernity gave us new translations, back to the sources of the scriptures; postmodernity gave us a context in which to understand Jesus, whom others believed him to be, and who he believed himself to be. Integral thought gives us a full picture of how the magic in the story enticed those at magical thinking, how the mythic in the tradition gave structure to those at mythic, and so on, through the ages and stages up until our own. Our understanding and appreciation of the world's religions have grown too; it was less than 60 years ago that the Catholic Church, for one, admitted "salvation" to adherents of other religions, and in fact sang their praises in the Vatican II encyclical

Nostra Aetate. The world's religions have illuminated my own way with their lanterns, unique and precious. Throughout this book and on our journey together, I'll draw from those lanterns, East and West, and from the lights of contemporary culture and Integral thought, all of which illuminate the power and majesty of the realization of Christ in history, Christ in mystery. If Christ is the Alpha, Christ too is the Omega; it is the Omega that pulls us toward herself, and the kingdom has come very close.

In this light, we begin with the early, sublime words of Advaita Vedanta Hinduism, from the great sage Shankara, and echoed closer to our time by Ramana Maharshi: "the world is illusory." This signpost marks the trailhead at the beginning of the spiritual journey, East and West, and as we consider Jesus in history, it marks the beginning of his way. No sooner had he heard "You are my son, the beloved," then he was led by the Spirit into the wilderness.

And what of the wilderness? Ramana gave a simple practice—that of self-inquiry—to repeatedly ask: "who am I?" He instructed that if we continue to ask that question with ever more profound depth, ever more clear presence, we will eliminate all that we are not (but what we imagined ourselves to be, in our original sin of mistaken self-identity), and Awareness alone will remain: that *I Am*. The practice is *neti, neti* (not this, not that) followed unto Awareness itself. Once all else is left behind, the nature of Awareness is *Satchitananda:* Being, Consciousness, Bliss. This knowledge Maharshi called *jnana-drishti*—seeing through the eye of knowledge, in profound intuition—as opposed to *jagat-drishti*, our ordinary perception of the world, which Maharshi considered a superimposition atop that which alone is: "I."

Contemporary philosopher Ken Wilber shared a sublime teaching around deep spiritual practice, East and West. The teaching is the "Three Faces of God," and the insight is simply this: as Ultimate Spirit—Awareness, by any other name—manifests, it manifests as three faces, depending on the perspective from which Spirit is experienced. If we experience Spirit within and as our own consciousness, as our deepest Self, we know Spirit in 1st-person. If we experience Spirit as a great "Thou" to whom we bring our deepest "I," we know Spirit in 2nd-person. If we experience Spirit in creation, recognizing Spirit dancing as *Lila* behind the external forms we see, we know Spirit in

3rd-person. Put simply, we can speak *as* Spirit, we can speak *to* Spirit, or we can speak *about* Spirit. Many of the great traditions through the centuries saw (only) one of these three faces of God; wars have been fought over which was the right face, and the raging theological debates of the future can be resolved simply by stepping back and noticing which face is coming to the fore, and consciously presencing the others.

The Three Faces of God are beautifully captured by Meister Eckhart, who taught that *even the Trinity* emerges, and it does so from God beyond God, God beyond description, or *Godhead*. The *Satchitananda* that alone remains at the end of the *via negativa* (I am not this, not that) is a perfect parallel to the Trinity that emerges from Godhead. As we see in the life of Jesus, as he beholds and then holds these three faces, he begins to manifest them in supremely powerful words and actions. As singer-songwriter Stuart Davis observed, "Godhead gives good phenomena."

Jesus, in the perception of John, experiences himself as the beloved "I" in relationship with a great "Thou" as Martin Buber wrote; he has seen the second face of God. Here we see the presence of the Holy Spirit as well (which, Father Thomas used to quip, "incidentally, is *not* a dove."). So we see three *external* elements of the Trinity at his baptism: the *Spirit* descending and remaining upon Jesus as he comes up out of the water, and the *Father*'s voice heard to say, "you (*Son*) are the beloved." This is such an important event that the Orthodox Church calls the feast *Theophany* (the manifestation of a deity in an observable way), and celebrates it with no less solemnity than Jesus' nativity.

The Theophany was a profound *state* of consciousness—a sublime occurrence experienced in 1st-person perspective, from within. In the wake of Jesus, there was a prolific flourishing of Western mysticism, superbly chronicled by Evelyn Underhill in her 1911 classic *Mysticism*. Wilber writes extensively on this movement through states of consciousness—waking, dreaming, deep sleep—which each of us journey through every night, and the ever-present state of *suchness* in which they arise, whether we bring our awareness to them or not.

The goal of spiritual practice, East and West, is to extend our *wakefulness* (what we are conscious of) from the waking state to the dream state to the state of deep sleep, and beyond that, to the ever-present state which underlies them all. In stabilizing these *states*, we consciously embody the gross, subtle, and causal energies (or literally, "bodies") that support those states. At each switchpoint of our growth through states, we acquire a new *vantage point* from which to experience reality, and at each, we come into a deeper identity (ego, soul, Self, suchness). The journey we undertake each night as we sleep forms the basis and foretaste of our lifetime's direct and deepening spiritual experience. And the good news is the possibility to awaken to Awareness through all of them.

But what of the experience of Jesus Himself? What can we know about his own experience of the divine, quite apart from centuries of theology proposed about him? We hear John declare him the son of God; we hear Peter proclaim him to be the Messiah. But who do we say that he is, given twenty centuries of reflection? And who did he believe himself to be?

Given modern methodologies, going back to sources and the careful reading of books contemporaneous to the Bible, we can see with clarity that Jesus too journeyed through these states and progressively stabilized them, coming ever more deeply from who he believed himself to be. We see in his baptism the *awakening of the self* of Underhill; in the Gospels of Matthew, Mark, and Luke, Jesus sees the heavens opened and the Spirit descending upon him. Of note, the writer of the Gospel of John records the Baptist, too, as seeing the Spirit descend and remain on Jesus; the state of Jesus, at his baptism, is so profound as to evoke the state of awakening in the Baptist as well.

Immediately following his baptism, Jesus is "led by the Spirit into the wilderness," and he undergoes Underhill's *purification of the self.* There Jesus fasts for forty days and is tempted by the devil. He emerges from the desert "filled with the power of the Spirit." By the time he emerges from the wilderness and begins to move in the world for a scarcely believable three-year ministry—given its impact on subsequent world history and the very direction of evolution—he has already embarked upon Underhill's next state-stage, the *illumination of the self.* Here we see a number of profound movements in Jesus' practice: he begins to relate to all three faces of God, and he begins to inhabit these faces from the inside.

Before Abraham Was, I Am

oing into the wilderness, Jesus had attained a high state of consciousness of the second face of God (when he was found in the temple in Jerusalem at 12 years of age, he asked his parents "Did you not know that I must be in my Father's house?"). What is interesting is that *coming out* of the wilderness, he has seen the first face of God: when questioned about Abraham, he responds "before Abraham was, I Am," directly echoing the name that Israel's God gave to Moses when Moses asked, to the effect of "whom shall I say is calling?" This name of God is YHWH, and the God that Moses encountered is the God beyond all description: simply "I Am who Am." Here, Jesus is speaking unmistakably *as* Spirit.

Interestingly—and this is a theme we shall see throughout—Moses is so taken aback (and so early in the history of spiritual practice) that he is unable to contain the immensity of the experience of God in his 1st-person perspective, and so he projects and perceives that experience in his 3rd-person perspective, in a burning bush outside of himself, ablaze but never consumed. Jesus encounters the same God that Moses had, but interprets and expresses that experience by stating "before Abraham was, I Am." Even more surprisingly, he doesn't say "before Abraham was, I was," thus claiming to have existed prior to Abraham in time. He says "I Am," indicating that he *Is*, always already, in a moment outside of time, and thus present for all of time.

Even as Jesus deepens his experience of the divine, He gazes upon (and increasingly, looks through) this first face of God. The external elements of the Trinity, seen at his baptism, begin to manifest inside the person of Jesus, who realized his Christ self (the Second Person of the Trinity) and was evermore deeply in communion with the First and the Third Persons of the Trinity; ever more realizing *Dharmakaya, Nirmanakaya,* and *Sambhogakaya,* from a Buddhist perspective; ever more moving as Advaita Vedanta's *Being, Consciousness, Bliss.* The same Spirit that "overshadowed" Mary at Jesus' conception and descended upon and remained with him at his baptism calls him into the wilderness; that same Spirit fills him with power on emerging from the wilderness. In his first recorded sermon in Luke's Gospel, he quotes from Isaiah: "The Spirit of the Lord is upon me," and then rolls up the scroll and proclaims, "this scripture today is fulfilled, in your midst." At thirty years of age, his ministry begins, and the "Spirit" has clearly been with him from the beginning.

Throughout that ministry, we find a remarkable rhythm of contemplation and action, illumination and embodiment. He is conscious of his involution, and from the *gnosis* gained from the journey, he moves fearlessly in his evolution. He flashes forth from "Jesus with the children" to "Christ in the Temple" with no hesitation. After the multiplication of the loaves, Jesus "went up on the mountain to pray." Right before choosing his apostles, "he went into the hills to pray, and all night he continued in prayer to God." He "came down from the mountain" to calm the storm and walk on the water. Before his momentous question "who do you say that I am?" in which Peter recognized Christ in Jesus, he was "praying alone." Before he taught his apostles the prayer *Our Father*, "he was praying in a certain place." He spent the night on the Mount of Olives just prior to saying "let the one who has not sinned cast the first stone," and declaring "before Abraham was, I Am." Before raising Lazarus from the dead, Jesus prayed. In the Garden of Gethsemane, the night before dying for love, he spent the night in prayer. Jesus prayed "without ceasing," cultivating a state imbued with the power and wisdom of God. His path down the mountain ever led to the stilling of the waters and drawing the line in the sand.

I and the Father Are One

Christianity is typically thought of as primarily a 2nd-person approach to Spirit, and Jesus' life is replete with references to his relationship with the Father. He uses the Aramaic word "Abba" which until that point had never been used as a name of God, and must have been scandalous to his listeners. *Abba* was an affectionate term that children of all ages, and especially little children, used for their fathers; it's best translated as "Papa" or "Daddy." In the Garden of Gethsemane, speaking directly *to* Spirit, Jesus prays:

> Abba, Father, for you all things are possible; remove this cup from me; yet, not what I want, but what you want. (Mark 14:36)

Jesus from a young age encountered the transcendent God as immanent; he speaks constantly of his relationship with the Father, and of the revelations borne of that relationship. Notably, he states "before Abraham was, I Am" *before* revealing that "I and the

Father are one." Thus Jesus bore the first face of God *and then merged it* with the second Face. For Jesus, God is relationship, and that relationship is known from within. He not only enters into intimate relationship with God—moreover, he *embodies* it.

Consider the Lilies

The 1st- and 2nd-person-perspectives on Spirit— the very faces of God—were seen by Jesus, and ever more deeply, he himself looked through them. But he saw through the third face as well.

Jesus frequently teaches *about* Spirit. He refers to the kingdom of God 68 times in the New Testament, and to the kingdom of heaven 32 times. Coming from a profound, stabilized state of consciousness, he describes the outer world as the perfect reflection of his inner realized state. The world he describes is the "new earth" of John the Evangelist's book of Revelation:

> Then I saw a new heaven and a new earth; for the first heaven and the first earth had passed away. (Revelation 21:1)

The new heaven is Jesus' realized *state*; the new earth is its perfect reflection as form, as matter. The world is described in the terms that he used in his inaugural sermon: the good news is brought to the poor, the captives are released, the blind regain their sight, the oppressed go free, all because the Spirit of the Lord was upon him. Jesus describes the third face of God which is "on earth as it is in heaven," the kingdom of heaven that has come in Israel's midst, by Jesus' *illumination*. Jesus confirms this when John—the Baptist who beheld the Spirit descend and remain with him—who had been arrested, hears of Jesus' works and sends his disciples to inquire whether Jesus was the promised one of the prophet Isaiah. Jesus tells them:

> Go and tell John what you hear and see: the blind receive their sight, the lame walk, the lepers are cleansed, the deaf hear, the dead are raised, and the poor have good news brought to them. (Luke 7:22)

Jesus regards and then inhabits the third face of God, enacting an exterior, new earth as a perfect reflection of the interior, new heaven of his illumination, his stabilized state: the kingdom of heaven.

From the early days of his mission, Jesus demonstrates a familiarity and a communion with the elements. His first miracle is to turn water into wine at the wedding at Cana. The Gospels of Matthew, Mark, and Luke record Jesus calming the seas; Matthew, Mark, and John record Jesus walking on the waters of the Sea of Galilee to the apostles' boat, and even empowering Peter to do the same. If there was ever a gesture that revealed his dust to Divinity, it was when a man blind from birth was brought to him to test Jesus ("who sinned, this man or his parents, that he was born blind?"). Spitting on the ground, Jesus bends down to make a paste from the earth, which he applies to the man's eyes; he sends the man to wash in the Pool of Siloam ("sent") and there the man regains his sight. The Psalms have been called "the garden of the contemplative," and here Jesus the contemplative—having spent the night in the garden—embodies God, as in Psalm 113:

> There is none like our God in the heavens or on earth *who lifts the poor from the dust* seating them with the mighty *who stoops to raise the weak and low*; may the Lord be praised, praise to the name of the Lord.

Jesus uses the lowest of elements, dirt, to divinely give sight to the blind. In the Sermon on the Mount, Jesus invites his listeners:

Consider the lilies of the field, how they grow; they neither toil nor spin, yet I tell you, even Solomon in all his glory was not clothed like one of these. (Matthew 6:29)

Here Jesus is doing much more than asking his listeners to think for a moment about lilies. Rather, he as *Consciousness* has known and loved the lilies, and considered how they—the *Bliss* that is creation—are considered by his Father—the *Being* who is creator. Thomas Merton says

> The forms and individual characters of living and growing things, of inanimate beings, of animals and flowers and all nature, constitute their holiness in the sight of God. Their inscape is their sanctity. It is the imprint of His wisdom and His reality in them…. The pale flowers of the dogwood outside this window are saints. The little yellow flowers that nobody notices on the edge of that road are saints looking up into the face of God.[1]

Jesus' sermon has echoes of the Flower Sermon of Zen Buddhism—in Chinese, *Niān huá wéi xiào*, literally, "pick up flower, subtle smile"—in which the Buddha transmits direct *prajñā* (wisdom) to his disciple Mahākāśyapa. Jesus too "picked up flower, subtle smile"; he gave transmission too. As he concludes his sermon, "the crowds were astounded at his teaching, for he taught them as one having authority, and not as their scribes." His *authority* is in his union with the *Author*, the Painter who adorned the lilies more majestically than Israel's king.

Jesus' first miracle—the water into wine, at the wedding at Cana—presaged one of his last, and definitive miracles: transforming bread and wine into the Body and Blood of Christ, saying "take this all of you, and eat it, drink it; this is my body and blood, given for you." It can be tempting to consider this a symbolic teaching, but Saint Pio of Pietrelcina points out that Jesus, earlier in John's Gospel, speaks in increasingly visceral terms of the literal teaching—even as many disciples turn away—saying whoever "gnaws" (in the sense of how a dog gnaws on a bone) on his flesh remains in him, and he in her. Having said this, Jesus later takes bread and wine (which earth has given and human hands have made, from earth's elements) and proclaims it his body and blood. The vastness of his mind is reflected by the vastness of his body: the earth is his body, the earth his blood. He is living the *Heart Sutra*; his form is not other than emptiness, and his emptiness, not other than form. And as his earthly ministry enters its last days, he takes on the three faces of God—now as *I Am who Am*, now as the beloved Son, now as one with creation, with the lilies of the field, with bread and wine, with the world, his body, and the kingdom of heaven, his heart.

We'll consider miracles more deeply as we journey, but this point must be made: Jesus' miracles *are not* the point. His message was *metanoia*; his message was transformation. When his followers marveled at the miraculous, he continually pointed beyond; their purpose is "to get us on his wavelength" of the kingdom within, and the new earth without. When he foresaw Nathaniel, one of his first apostles, in an inexplicably prescient way, Jesus said to him:

> Do you believe because I told you that I saw you under the fig tree? You will see greater things than these." And he said to him, "Very truly, I tell you, you will see heaven opened and the angels of God ascending and descending upon the Son of Man. (John 1:50-51)

Our modern scholarship can most definitely critique the literal truth of some of these miracles (though it can't dismiss them entirely, any more than it can dismiss the inexplicable phenomena of our own time; see Michael Murphy, *The Future of the Body*); we are primarily interested in Jesus' state of consciousness, the trail of embodied love that he blazed, and the footsteps he left for us to follow as we embody love no less than did he.

The Kingdom at Hand

We have seen how Jesus deepened his realization, from his *awakening* as a child of twelve being lost and then found in "his Father's house," to a man coming up out of the Jordan, the Son spoken of by the Father and touched by the Spirit. Driven by the Spirit into the wilderness, his *purgation* and *illumination* take place. Out of the wilderness, he has internalized even the Trinity, who had been seen from the outside at his Baptism. Now they are seen from inside: looking through his 1st-person perspective, "before Abraham was, I Am." Looking through his 2nd-person perspective, "I and the Father are one." Looking through his 3rd-person perspective, he takes bread, which human hands have made, and wine, the fruit of the earth, to be his body, and gives them as such. As he deepens his *illumination*, he knows God from within; rather than

31

looking *at* God, he looks *as* God, and the three faces beheld become the three faces from which to behold. This is the kingdom of heaven that John foretold and that Jesus proclaimed. The kingdom, said Jesus, was not something that could be observed, because "the kingdom is within." In the wilderness, the Consciousness of Christ, in the mind and body of Jesus, abides in Awareness, until, as Meister Eckhart—from whom God hid nothing—knew:

> "The eye through which I see God is the same eye through which God sees me; my eye and God's eye are one eye, one seeing, one knowing, one love." [2]

Peter, in answer to Jesus' question "who do you say that I am?" replies "the Messiah," and Jesus says "truly I tell you, some who are standing here will not taste death until they see the kingdom of God." Eight days thereafter, in a perfect bookend to his baptism, Jesus ascends a mountain with Peter, James, and John (the "some standing here") and while praying, is transfigured: his face shines like the sun, his clothes become dazzling white, and he appears with Moses and Elijah in splendor. The Father, echoing the words spoken at Jesus' baptism, declares

This is my Son, the Beloved; with him I am
well pleased; listen to him! (Matthew 17:5)

In that moment, they behold Jesus as he truly Is,
and see the kingdom as Jesus foretold; they have seen
the kingdom before tasting death. The kingdom that
Jesus preached was not to come at the chronological
end of this world, or in a revolution against Roman
rule; the kingdom is profoundly realized in Jesus' state,
and indeed is in their midst.

As Jesus' public ministry reaches its apex, he is
apparently hell-bent toward Jerusalem and the Temple, and on a collision course with the political and
religious leaders of his time and place. His sermons
become increasingly concerned with end-of-times references (e.g. the parable of the last judgement) and he
increasingly references himself as a king. In the wake
of raising Lazarus, he arrives in Jerusalem for the Passover in his 33rd year, and he is welcomed as a king;
the people of Jerusalem line his way and bear palms
to salute his triumphant entry: the King of the Jews.

Following the last supper in Jerusalem, Jesus, too,
experiences Underhill's *dark night of the soul* that so
many in his footsteps came to know. He and his disciples go to a place called Gethsemane, and he says

to Peter, James and John: "I am deeply grieved, even to death," and throwing himself on the ground, prays three times—with such intensity that "his sweat became like great drops of blood falling down on the ground"—"Father, if it is possible, let this cup pass from me; yet, not my will but yours be done."

What happened next might have been the end of it. Jesus is taken by the Temple guards, chief priests and elders; he is judged by Pilate, and—though his wife knew of Jesus' innocence in a dream—he is sentenced to death. On the cross he forgives those who crucified him—"they know not what they do"—and quotes the twenty-second Psalm "my God, my God, why have you abandoned me?" before commending his Spirit (with him, from beginning to end) and breathing his last. We are told that, though it was mid-afternoon, darkness fell upon the land, and the darkest of dark nights fell upon Jesus of Nazareth.

Though the state-stages of the East and the West parallel one another beautifully, the Eastern flavor of nonduality has only recently been tasted, with relatively few exceptions, in the West. To the question of whether Jesus' words reveal a nondual realization, there has been some debate. In my estimation, his proclamation that "before Abraham was, I Am" and *then* "I and the Father are one" speaks powerfully of not only the Father but of the Godhead beyond God; the "I" of his statement was the realized, divine Christ, so *the "one" was beyond them both.* His words to his apostles at his last supper are a sublime declaration of Oneness of all that is. But if his teachings are nondual, his greater teaching, his life, was unmistakably "not two." His task in his every moment was to bridge the seeming divide between heaven and earth—perfectly wedded in his heart—with love, of which he had an inexhaustible Source. "Though he was in the form of God," he launched himself into the heart of suffering with reckless abandon; by the time he gets to Jerusalem—with his "destroy this Temple and I will rebuild it in three days—it becomes clear that the town isn't big enough for the two of them: Jesus and the Temple. His profound words are eclipsed by his mystical deeds.

Jesus' gesture with bread and wine at his last supper was a supremely powerful action—perhaps more than we have yet realized. In it, he comes from a state of such *suchness* that he gives bread and wine—*everything on the table*, "which earth has given and human hands have made"—as his very body. (Even as he lost many disciples in his earlier teaching "I am the Bread of Life," he doubled down on the importance and literal truth of his message.) The inner state that Jesus had realized—the kingdom of heaven—is reflected perfectly in the earth, made new in a moment outside of time, blessed, broken and given to all. In this singular gesture he overcomes the primordial dualities of interior and exterior, individual and collective, in "the new and everlasting covenant." In love, Jesus gives us the Body of Christ, just as in love, we become Kahlil Gibran's "sacred bread for God's sacred feast."

The Catholic Church teaches that only those baptized Catholic can receive communion, but a beautiful friend of mine whispered an astonishing insight: "I don't need to take the bread and wine to receive the Body and Blood." The Catholic Church teaches that the bread and wine become Christ's body and blood through the miracle of transubstantiation; but I say to you, he transubstantiates space and time, as the Earth's gifts become the Infinite and Eternal Body of Christ, in the new and everlasting covenant that is always already here and now, through the depth and presence of Jesus.

And the greater miracle is the man himself, who looked all the way up and beheld a God who looked all the way down to behold the man, to commune where, as ever, heaven and earth come together—in the most Sacred Heart of Christ. As St. Paul wrote to the Philippians:

> And though he was in the form of God, Jesus did not deem equality with God something to be taken advantage of; rather he emptied himself, taking the form of a slave, coming in human likeness, and found in human appearance, he humbled himself, becoming obedient to death, even death on a cross. (Philippians 2:6-8)

Jesus emptied himself—of ego, soul, Self and suchness—in a profound life of *kenosis* (in Greek: self-giving) and in doing so, discovered his Christhood. The last thing he did in his early life was to give up his Spirit, just before giving up his body. With his Divinity came a radical *freedom* to convene the kingdom of God, to walk on earth as the very fulfillment that Moses and Elijah pointed to, to make of his own body an everlasting Temple, in the shadow of the earthly temple that was soon to be destroyed. To accomplish, as a human being, what was promised and long-expected of Israel's God. When the Word became flesh, the transcendent God became imminent, and the kingdom drew near. The two commandments which summed up the Law and the Prophets ("Love the Lord your God with all your heart, and all your mind, and all your soul, and all your strength, and love your neighbor as your self") he lived perfectly, but deepening his identity of self, he found himself, as Christ, in all things: the least of his sisters and brothers, and even considering the lilies. His neighbour thus became everyone and indeed, all sentient beings.

Early on the morning of the third day, Mary of Magdala—she who stood at the foot of his cross and never turned away—came to the tomb in which Jesus had been laid, with a jar of myrrh to anoint his body, as when burying one's beloved, in the custom of the day. To her astonishment, the stone had been rolled away, and the body was gone. The linen wrappings lay on the floor of the tomb, but the cloth that had covered his head had been rolled up neatly and set aside, as if to say (as when dining, in the custom of the day): "I'm not finished...."

Two
FULLY HUMAN

It can seem a long time since Jesus' "hasty visit and our brief welcome," in Gibran's words. Twenty centuries have fallen, like a patina on the tomb. The dusty roads of ancient Palestine can seem remote from our information superhighway, and the universe of Jesus distant from the metaverse of today.

But twenty centuries can also bring new lenses to see through, and clarity to see with. Informed by contemporary scholarship, we can dare to take the perspective of Jesus—to learn the context he moved in, to better illuminate the content of his words and his actions. In this day and age, his followers are called not only to follow in his footsteps, but also to walk a mile in his sandals. And in doing so, the light of his life might shine in a new way upon our own.

The stages of consciousness are one such modern

insight that can help us understand the life of Jesus in a new way. Whereas the states of consciousness are as old as humanity itself, and have laid out our spiritual journey for as long, stages were spotted relatively recently—within the last century—and form an entirely different trajectory that we also navigate through our life's journey. The stages of consciousness are laid down by evolution, and every human being starts at square one. While humanity's earlier stages are relatively invariant at this point, its later stages are, by contrast, relatively undefined. Those that venture into the later states are quite literally blazing a trail for the rest who will follow, on the great journey back to Spirit.

Many different versions (or "lines") of these stage progressions have been articulated, each tracking the answers to a different, basic question over time. Who do you say that you are? Of what are you aware? What should you do? And crucially, in our case "What is of ultimate concern?" Ken Wilber has helpfully correlated more than a dozen of these lines of development through broad stages he refers to as *altitudes*. The stages of consciousness are a vital addition to our knowledge of human development because with each new stage a new *view* is given. And whatever we experience from the vantage point of our *state of consciousness*, we unpack and interpret through the view of our *stage of consciousness*.

Though their discovery is recent, stages of consciousness give us lenses with which to view the lives of those who've gone before us, and provide valuable insights for our own lives. (This is entirely different from projecting medieval Christologies onto Jesus; the stages *subsisted* in Jesus' time, just as atoms did. They did not yet properly *exist*, since no one yet knew of them.) Jesus, *fully divine*—who through *awakening, purgation, illumination, dark night* and *union*, became one with God, and embodied the Torah, the Temple and God's promised return—was also *fully human*. He experienced his state of consciousness, the very kingdom of God, from his stage of consciousness, and the lenses of a semetic man at the dawn of the common era. What can we know then, of his stage of consciousness?

Developmentalists track six to eight major stages to have unfolded thus far in human history (to give one example, Jean Gebser's archaic, magic, mythic, mental, integral); these stages can be grouped into three major tiers (e.g., 1st-tier, 2nd-tier, 3rd-tier). At the time of Jesus, the mythic stage was the leading edge, with mental, integral and beyond yet to emerge; so beyond the personal tier that ended with mythic was a momentous leap into the trans-mythic, a trail that had yet to be blazed. Those who pushed that leading edge would have found themselves in an undiscovered country, and uncharted waters. Their very footsteps on new ground became the paths upon which later human beings would find their way, in ways that we now assume to be "given."

The *stages of consciousness* are of crucial importance because they are the lenses through which we view, unpack, and interpret our *states of consciousness*. We saw that Jesus attained a high realization, or illumination, of oneness with the Father, whom he knew intimately as "Abba." Now, with the benefit of modern scholarship, we can attempt to strap his sandals on our feet and walk a mile in them, to try to understand what his context was and who he believed himself to be. Having some understanding of his *vantage point* (awakened, illuminated then in union with God) through *states*, we can begin to understand the *view* he took through *stages*: the hidden map of meaning that we can discern twenty centuries later.

The Parable of Spirit's Dive

In the day, Ken Wilber shared what now seems like a parable that the Master might have shared to those who gathered around at the profundity of his words—a parable of involution and evolution, and the spiritual journey of humanity, with the number of transmigrants, as Shankara held, to be *exactly one*. By involution, Spirit *involves* itself as manifestation, in a moment outside of time. Advaita Vedanta holds there to be three great arcs of involution and evolution: the arc of Spirit becoming form in the Cosmic Inflation of the Big Bang, and the resulting 14 billion year (and counting) evolutionary journey back to Spirit; the involution of a human lifetime, as Divinity becomes dust, which then evolves toward Divinity (and wakes up and starts writing poetry, Wilber quipped) until its death; and our every breath, as Spirit fills and informs us as we inhale, and we reach out and return to Spirit as we exhale.

Regarding the first great arc, Spirit, said Wilber, was like a bungee jumper, jumping off a bridge across a beautiful valley, with an enormous canvas hung from the bridge, on which is painted a picture of that same valley. At the lowest point of the descent of involution, a human being is conceived, a precious human birth takes place, and a precious human life begins. Spirit as that jumper experiences the valley by viewing the painting, from the low point in the jump and through the evolution of rebounding back up toward the bridge. In most cases the jumper will experience life as we know it, with all its pleasure and pain, wonder and devastation, and love, as given, determined, fate. But occasionally jumpers will come back with such force and momentum that they experience the top of the painting, and a blank canvas. At the same time, they open their eyes to the actual valley for the first time, like the early humans emerging from Plato's cave. And they fill the canvas with the view that they hold of the valley. Subsequent jumpers who reach that same height on their return will then see the new imagery the previous jumper had painted. That in fact is how the entire canvas is filled.

The jump is *involution*; the return is *evolution*; the same Spirit makes repeated jumps as unique sentient beings. On the jump and outside of our usual consciousness, Spirit descends through vast fields of potential (the great primordial *states* of consciousness); at the bottom of the jump, Spirit becomes conscious, endowed with a mind, and embodied. The jumper, now as a sentient being, returns on their evolutionary journey through the evolutionarily constructed *stages* of consciousness. They experience the early levels of development—really, just Kosmic habits—that are so well laid down as to seem somewhat invariant, even deterministic. But as the jumper gets higher and higher, the canvas is less complete; the levels less engraved in stone, and they discern the beginnings of the real view of the valley. The responsibility of the jumper is now profound. They are no longer simply experiencing an image of the valley painted by another hand; they are now witnessing the valley itself. And it falls to them to paint an image which will be experienced as reality by countless jumpers to follow. The future is in their hands.

Jesus, too, was one who made the jump; he took on the second set of Wilber's eight words: GROW UP. In his case he reached the blank canvas quite quickly, during his *illumination*. In three years of deeply loving, he filled the canvas with the tenderness and ferocity of that love, that are now his signature in the transpersonal realms.

Your Neighbour as Yourself

Contemporary biblical scholar N.T. Wright wrote of Jesus' understanding of himself that several themes would have been prominent: Torah and Temple, and the coming or return—as promised by Isaiah—of Israel's God, and God's right hand, the Messiah (the anointed). From this we can surmise that through Jesus' awakening and illumination he began to *situate* himself within these themes. And as we shall see, in the union of his death and beyond, he moved definitively to *fulfill* them in himself.

Jesus clearly loved the Torah, the Jewish scriptures, and knew them well. He traded scriptural references in debate with no less than the devil (!) during his time in the wilderness. In the early sermon on the mount, Jesus made clear that he had not come to abolish the Law, but to fulfill it. He unveiled a profoundly deeper understanding of the Law, in majestic cadence, of "you have heard it said...*but I say unto you...*" on six points in the Law, amazing his listeners by the authority with which he taught, unlike the teachers of the Law. He ferociously defended the spirit of the Law, even when treading on the letter (to outraged accusations of "this man heals on the Sabbath!"). His

first recorded teaching in Luke's Gospel begins with
the reading of the scroll of Isaiah:

> "The Spirit of the Lord is upon me, because
> he has anointed me to bring good news to the
> poor. He has sent me to proclaim release to the
> captives and recovery of sight to the blind, to
> let the oppressed go free, to proclaim the year
> of the Lord's favor." and, with every eye in the
> synagogue fixed on him, he said "today this
> scripture is fulfilled in your midst," amazing
> those who listened. (Luke 4:18)

Time and time again through the Gospels, we see
Jesus discussing with the learned of his day, and evad-
ing every scriptural trap set for him. "Whose image
do you see on this coin? Render unto Caesar...." "Let
the one who has not sinned cast the first stone...."
He answered with such deep insight and compassion,
such clarity and vision, that "they dared question him
no more." We see, too, Jesus moving consciously to
fulfill scripture, not in words but in his very deeds, so
that only afterward, those who marvelled at his life,
his death, saw in him the perfect fulfillment of all that
had been promised.

The Temple, too, was a constant theme in the life
of Jesus. We read of his being presented there as a baby,

in Simeon's arms ("Lord, now you let your servant go in peace.") We hear of his parents going to Jerusalem every year for the Festival of the Passover, and after going missing when he was twelve, Jesus being found in the Temple, sitting among the teachers, listening to them and asking them questions. We see him enraged at the moneychangers in the court of the Temple, turning their tables and driving them out. When asked for a sign to prove his authority for doing so, he replied, "destroy this Temple and I will raise it again in three days." John tells us that Jesus was speaking of the Temple of his body; and he who was made flesh and "tabernacled" among us raised the mystical Temple of his body as well.

The third of N.T. Wright's themes was the coming and return of Israel's God, as promised in Isaiah. Israel was amidst the *Second Temple* period; the feeling in Israel was that her God had withdrawn, and was no longer actively involved in her history. The Romans were present there, in an uneasy truce, and Jerusalem was a powderkeg: like the Capitol riot, and then some. The promise of Isaiah was that Israel's God would return in a powerful way, with many prophecies of a foreseen Messiah, the right hand of God, who would lead her to the forefront of the nations of earth.

We can see, then, Jesus at the leading edge of Jewish society in its own culture war with the occupying Romans, Israel trying to regain its own mythic sovereignty, and Rome attempting to assert its own at a global scale (in the known world of the time). Jesus' very condemnation at the hands of Roman governor Pontius Pilate was to avoid a riot, and Caiphas had presciently said that "it was better for one man to die…."

But the one who blazed these trails at the leading edge of development also went quite beyond. In the "mind of Christ" was a different sort of knowing, and a different sort of loving. When he summed up the Law and the Prophets, he did so in a two-fold instruction of love: "you shall love the Lord God with all your heart, and all your mind, and all your soul, and all your strength. And you shall love your neighbor as yourself." The Law and the Prophets all come down to love, and love incarnate lived and died to share that Good News.

In the first commandment to love (you shall love the Lord your God with all your heart, and all your mind, and all your soul, and all your strength), we see that Jesus himself practiced what he preached: he loved God with his Sacred Heart, with his Christic mind, in the totality of his bodymind (soul), and with the strength to endure death on a cross, with his final words forgiving those who killed him and quoting a Psalm that was fulfilled in its very speaking. He loved God and neighbour as he commanded, and with his final breath, set upon the winds eternal and infinite compassion, to every time and place.

The second commandment was like the first, to love neighbor as self. But notice, the self had become Christ in all beings, the least of his sisters and his brothers, the lilies of the field. And neighbor had become all humans—as Elijah was sent to a widow in Sidon, and Elisha, a leper in Syria—and the good Samaritan took in the man who fell upon robbers on the road to Jericho. In speaking to his apostles at his last supper, Jesus gave a new commandment: again, a commandment to love. "Love one another as I have loved you." His summary of the groundbreaking monotheistic tradition of Judaism always came down to one word (there is no better word, if we understand it): love.

In the mind of Christ, we see consciousness turned toward Awareness, and Awareness beholding consciousness; Jesus perfectly enacts what Meister Eckhart would articulate twelve centuries later:

> The eye through which I see God is the same eye through which God sees me; my eye and God's eye are one eye, one seeing, one knowing, one love.[1]

It was this Awareness, through Christ Consciousness, that animated the mind and body of Jesus, and through which he knew and loved all beings, perfect reflections of the transcendent God and immanent God-with-us.

Love, Knowledge, Liberation

Such knowledge is universal and Kosmic, and is known beautifully in the East. Ramana Maharshi instructed those who sought the divine to practice self inquiry: to ask "who am I?" deeply, repeatedly, seeing through all the veils of who we are not, but mistakenly identified ourselves with, in what was truly our original sin. When all the views have fallen away, says Ramana, all that is left is *Satchitananda*—in another translation: Being, Knowing, Loving. Jesus' realization was "I Am," and therefore "I Am that."

When viewed from twenty centuries away, and in

the light of these radiant lanterns of the East, we see in the life of Jesus an amazing, conscious movement from Being, in the lonely places in the early morn, to Knowing, as he taught in the synagogues, to Loving, as he proclaimed good news to the poor, release to the captives, sight to the blind, freedom to the oppressed, and fulfilled the words of the scroll of Isaiah: "the Spirit of the Lord is upon me."

The *knowing* of Jesus is frequently referred to in the Gospels. Rather than the omniscience of transcendent Awareness (which we can easily project onto Jesus, and often have), his knowing has the character of the immanent Christ Consciousness, and resembles the "personal omniscience" that Ken Wilber finds in the later stages of development. Every moment is embraced, known intuitively from within, and therefore loved:

> When he was in Jerusalem during the Passover festival, many believed in his name because they saw the signs that he was doing. But Jesus on his part would not entrust himself to them, because he knew all people and needed no one to testify about anyone; for he himself knew what was in everyone. (John 2:23-25)

As Jesus shares his last supper with his apostles, they exclaim:

Now we know that you know all things, and
do not need to have anyone question you; by
this we believe that you came from God. (John
16:30)

And Peter, who three times said "I am not," even
as Jesus spoke "I Am" to Pilate, replied to his question,
asked three times, "do you love me?':

Lord, you know everything; you know that I
love you. (John 21:17)

Jesus recognized Christ within, and recognized
his Christ self within his sisters and brothers, and
loved them as such. He knew and loved by *gnosis*:
"knowledge or insight into humanity's real nature as
divine, leading to the deliverance of the divine spark
within humanity from the constraints of earthly existence." The knowledge of the mind of Christ corresponds perfectly to *jnana-drishti*, one of Hinduism's
great paths to *moksha*, liberation.

Contemporary Advaita master Sri Nisargadatta
Maharaj also speaks of this knowledge, this love:

When you realize that you are the light of the
world, you will also realize that you are the love of
it; that to know is to love and to love is to know.[2]

And again:

I find that somehow, by shifting the focus of attention, I become the very thing I look at and experience the kind of consciousness it has; I become the inner witness of the thing. I call this capacity of entering other focal points of consciousness—love.[3]

With twenty centuries of retrospect, we can lose the sense of how shocking the words of Jesus must have been; what sound today like Sunday School teachings of being nice to one another were revolutionary in his day. But they were evolutionary too. We see in the mind of Christ the hallmarks of the radically new trans-mythic stages, beyond the mythic leading edge of his time. Even in our time, these stages are relatively new, but Wilber traces some of the first outlines of them.

We see in the life of Jesus the realization of his nature as Christ Consciousness so totally that in him, Jesus experienced divinity even as Christ experienced humanity. Wilber, on this interweaving:

...the wholeness of 3rd tier, where wholeness becomes more directly interconnected and intermeshed with individual identity itself in a complex interweaving.[4]

His divinity is woven, through and through,

with his humanity, so that after twenty centuries, we still can't agree on who he was, and who he is. In the words of Gibran's man from Lebanon, nineteen centuries afterward, Jesus was "a man too weak and infirm to be God, a God too much man to call forth adoration." Wilber notes, too, of the emergence of superhuman capacities in the later levels of development:

> ...it is an Indra's Net electrically hyper charged with superhuman capacities in its every movement, as human and Divine become increasingly hard to tell apart, both dimensions seamlessly entangled with each other, as each other.[5]

We noted that the miracles of Jesus were never the point; the point was *transformation*. Magical stories captivated minds at the magical stage of development. But given Jesus' venture beyond the mythic-literal developmental edge of his day, the miracles he performed point to a superhuman capacity; there were twenty-two recorded healings in the Gospels of Matthew, Mark and Luke. While the rational level in us can dismiss them as myths, what look like laws to the rational are better understood as Kosmic habits laid down over millennia: paths well-traveled but not preordained or predestined. Even as the mythical worldviews of earlier stages can blind their adherents to rational truths, so too can a rational worldview blind us to transrational realities. Just as the Lucayan people who were indigenous to what is now known as the Bahamas likely could not even register the landfall of Columbus' ships on Guanahani Island, so we too can dismiss something plainly before our eyes if it does not fit into our worldview. We remain in Plato's cave, and refuse to leave, to turn our faces toward the sun. We prefer the comfort and familiarity of our own lenses and refuse to look through the telescope. We are, all of us, "in over our heads," as Robert Kegan titled his book on human development. We protest that miracles are impossible, but I say to you, in Boulding's First Law: anything that exists is possible.

From the view of Integral and beyond, Jesus' miracles are not the point. There is a deeper truth, if we can see it: the kingdom in our midst as an ever-present state, and a new earth as its perfect reflection, ours to enact, with the boundless love contained in the human heart. Oneness, notes Wilber, is also a prominent emergent theme in later stage development:

...all forms of spiritual intelligence at this indigo level have a strong focus on the communion of all being, or the interconnectedness and "oneness" of all sentient beings at all levels.[6]

We see a theme of oneness throughout the life of Jesus, so much that St. Julian of Norwich—one of the saints thought to have realized the nondual state— spoke of following Jesus as the way of "oneing." Jesus extends his knowing love to other races, to the least of his sisters and brothers, to the birds of the air and the flowers of the fields. At the last supper he prays that all may be one, even as he and his Father—transcendent Awareness and immanent Christ Consciousness—are one. In loving neighbor as self—not *as much as* self, but *as* self—Jesus teaches of and enacts this inter- connectedness, so that in his knowing and loving, the being of *Satchitananda* becomes the *interbeing* so beautifully proclaimed by Thich Nhat Hanh.

Jean Gebser's research is echoed in (or echoes) Jesus' transfiguration and his appearance to Mary of Magdala, who knew him best but scarcely recognized him following his resurrection, until his speaking of *Miriam*, her name. His giving of bread and wine— everything on the table—as truly his body and blood, is also reflected in his, in Wilber's words:

...luminous "visionary" awareness... feelings of
"shimmering," "gleaming," "incandescence,"
and "radiance"... and a profound sensing of the
surrounding environment as being one's own
body, one's own skin.[7]

Above all, we see in Jesus an unfailing intuition
from which he acted; always beginning from the "be
still, and know that I Am God" of the mountain, he
never hesitated in the drawing a line in the sand, or the
turning of the tables, as seen at Wilber's meta-mind:

...the type available at the meta-mind is a vari-
ety of spiritual intuition... a direct, immediate
perceiving or feeling.[8]

𝔗𝔥𝔢 𝔏𝔢𝔞𝔰𝔱 𝔬𝔣 𝔐𝔶 𝔖𝔦𝔰𝔱𝔢𝔯𝔰, 𝔅𝔯𝔬𝔱𝔥𝔢𝔯𝔰

The early teaching of "love your neighbour as
your self" is paralleled by "for where two or
three are gathered in my name, I Am there among
them," and is bookended by a late teaching, as Jesus
approaches Jerusalem, knowing that though his mission will not end well, nonetheless "all manner of
things shall be well." In one of his last teachings,

When the Son of Man comes in his glory, and
all the angels with him, then he will sit on the

throne of his glory. All the nations will be gathered before him, and he will separate people one from another as a shepherd separates the sheep from the goats, and he will put the sheep at his right hand and the goats at the left. Then the king will say to those at his right hand, "Come, you that are blessed by my Father, inherit the kingdom prepared for you from the foundation of the world; for I was hungry and you gave me food, I was thirsty and you gave me something to drink, I was a stranger and you welcomed me, I was naked and you gave me clothing, I was sick and you took care of me, I was in prison and you visited me." Then the righteous will answer him, "Lord, when was it that we saw you hungry and gave you food, or thirsty and gave you something to drink? And when was it that we saw you a stranger and welcomed you, or naked and gave you clothing? And when was it that we saw you sick or in prison and visited you?" And the king will answer them, "Truly I tell you, just as you did it to one of the least of these who are members of my family, you did it to me." (Matthew 25:31-40)

Here we see, again, the spaciousness of the true Self that Jesus has realized as a state—the vantage point—and the perspective, the view, of his stage. In the beginning, he taught his followers to love their neighbor as them selves; now he identifies *his very self* with the selves of the least of his sisters and brothers. He had spoken often enough about the birds of the air and the flowers of the field to be clear that the least of his sisters and brothers were the lowliest of all sentient beings. Christ consciousness in Jesus recognized, knew and loved Christ Consciousness in all beings.

The four Bodhisattva vows are:

Beings are numberless. I vow to save them.
Delusions are inexhaustible. I vow to end them.
Dharma gates are boundless. I vow to enter them.
Buddha's way is unsurpassable. I vow to be-
come it.

Jesus Christ, the Bodhisattva of Love, came to liberate all beings—they are the Sangha, the Bliss of *Satchitananda*, the Spirit. He was Manjushri to the Pharisees, cutting through their delusions, inexhaust-ible and exhausting. He himself said "I am the Gate," and was himself the Dharma, the Consciousness of *Satchitananda*, the Word. And if Jesus was the Gate, Christ is the Gateless Gate, seen from the other side, in the eyes of God. Jesus viewed God with the same eye with which God viewed Jesus, and Meister Eck-hart—from whom God hid nothing—knew that.

He himself proclaimed "I Am the Way," of Buddha, the Being of *Satchitananda*, the Father with whom he was one. And he walked in the West *as* the way, the way Gautama Buddha walked in the East. The Koran has it, "God's is the East, and God's is the West. Therefore look to the East and look to the West, and there you shall see the Face of God."

Metanoia

We see Jesus at the leading edge of the developmental stages that had unfolded in his day, and we see him going quite beyond, no longer following a trail but blazing one in love. His stage was trans-mythic, which corresponds to the *Supermind* of his day (the highest stage to have unfolded, to that time).

In Whitehead's description of time as a holarchy—with every moment prehending the previous moment and adding its novel emergent—Jesus' prehension of the moment was love, and he seems to have decided that the novel emergent too would be love, at times tender, at times ferocious, in and as every moment. Einstein is said to have called compound interest the "eighth wonder of the world." Imagine that the subject of every moment (who is Christ, our deepest self) becomes the object of the subject of the next moment (who is also Christ, but Christ anew) plus a novel emergent (which is love, to eternity and infinity). Imagine the immensity of that love, after Spirit's involutionary leap, and 14 billion years of evolution. Imagine a time in which the kingdom of heaven is within, a new earth is without, your mind is the mind of Christ—*metanoia*, the mind beyond mind—and your heart is the most Sacred Heart of Christ.

From there Jesus knew what to do, and no less than Pilate who judged him, nonetheless fell silent, washed his hands and stood there amazed. Jesus was fully human, and the stages of consciousness, seen twenty centuries later, demonstrate a life as unquestionably full as it was radically free.

Jesus' words and actions point so directly to post-leading edge awareness that one has to wonder whether that awareness actually points to Christ. Wilber speaks of certain apertures of Awareness, certain locuses of consciousness that so completely navigated the paths of states and stages that Spirit pours through them directly into form, unmediated by higher states and stages—because there are none—and taking form as pure possibility, with complete certainty. This is the

Spirit of Evolution, the subtitle of Wilber's master-piece *Sex, Ecology, Spirituality*. "The Spirit of the Lord is upon me," said Jesus at Nazareth, adding that "these words today are fulfilled in your midst." The Spirit of evolution was directly upon him, and flowed purely through him into form. He would have been among the first, East or West, to walk in that undiscovered country, and he took his sandals off, for he knew it to be Holy Ground. Perhaps the intuition of oneness—first dimly known in the Integral stages of consciousness, then lovingly enacted in the 3rd-tier stages—is imbued with love precisely due to the love of Christ that he imprinted there, a lantern in the still dark cathedral of being and an unmistakable signpost along the way to our future, an early realization of not only the Supermind of Christ but also his most Sacred Heart, fully human and fully divine.

Jesus was fully human; his aperture was open wide to those he came to, to those who came to him, to the Spirit who was upon him, the Father with whom he was one, and I Am, whom he knew himself to be. Even as his being fully divine reflects his *freedom*, so too does his being fully human reflect his *fullness*. He calls us to move from the mythical to the mystical. "Thy Kingdom come" is here and now—the only place and time we will ever have. "On earth as it is in heaven" is precisely the "emptiness is not other than form, form is not other than emptiness" that was known, by *jnana-drishti*, in the *Heart Sutra*.

Kahlil Gibran, when asked about the Immaculate Conception, responded "is not every conception immaculate?" and to the Church of his time, which had lost sight of Jesus' humanity, Gibran asked,

> And what consolation is there in a man like themselves, a man whose kindliness is like their own kindliness, a god whose love is like their own love, and whose mercy is in their own mercy?[9]

Jesus, too, had a precious human birth, and a precious human life. He was like us in every way, and thus, we are in every way like him. As God created the earth, in the lovely allegory of Genesis, God "saw that it was good." But when God created human beings, God "saw that it was *very* good."

THREE
LIGHT FROM LIGHT

The contemporary insight of *stages of development* is matched by an equally powerful and crucial insight: that of *shadow*. Given the two trajectories of human development, the ancient *states* that we navigate and the newly seen *stages* that we move through, much can go wrong, even in the best-case scenario. The very act of being born nearly kills us, and life doesn't get any easier; sometimes not all of the energy coalesced in one state or stage is ready to make the jump to the next.

Shadow, of course, is an ancient concept too. But contemporary insights on stage development and on how shadow can affect and impact both of our great journeys give us new lenses with which to view the life of Jesus.

While we—and Christianity itself—might have grown up with the image of Jesus as omniscient and omnipotent while on Mary's knee, modern scholarship reveals that Jesus, too, developed through states and stages, and if he was "like us in all things but sin," then he too would have encountered shadow in himself and others along the way. While the spark of Underhill's *illumination* was evidently with him through his childhood—seen in the finding in the Temple, at twelve—it was not yet aflame. His time in the wilderness, having been "led by the Spirit" following his baptism, led to his *illumination*. But it also was his time of *purgation*.

We read that Jesus fasted for forty days and forty nights in the desert—the genesis of the great season of Lent—and that he was tempted by the devil throughout. Once again, the view from the stages of modernity is quite different from the view in Jesus' day, and certainly from the writers of the Gospels. Just as the story of Moses and the burning bush can be seen now as a projection of the divine presence that the early Jewish leader could not bear within, and therefore saw without, the temptations of Jesus too can be seen in this light. The Gospels tell us only of three specific temptations at the end of the forty days; we are left to imagine what the others might have been.

Wilber's terms regarding shadow are deeply helpful here. Development into later states and stages involves transcending and including the earlier ones. When moving through both states and stages, we can develop an *addiction* to the elements of our current stage, or our current state (a failure to transcend). This addiction can then hold us back once we've otherwise sufficiently integrated that stage or state, and are ready to move on to the next. Conversely, we might develop an *allergy* to the elements of our current stage or state (a failure to include), disowning and dissociating from those elements.

As Robert Kegan noted, in the process of development, the subject of one stage becomes the object of the subject of the next stage. Wilber points out that in these transitions we are particularly vulnerable, such that the subject at one stage might refuse to become an object of the next stage, thus becoming a *subpersonality*. We are all a "legion" of personality and subpersonalities—parts that have split off through the switch-points of our state development and the fulcrums of our stage development. Part of our life-energy is spent maintaining these subpersonalities, and more still is spent keeping them repressed. Earlier subpersonalities can significantly distort our later personality; the distortions become increasingly catastrophic as we move toward later stages and states without having addressed our shadows—the parts of ourselves that have split off along the way. Most of us are a leaning tower of Pisa. That is why healthy spiritual development involves consciously navigating the ways of both states and stages, and consciously addressing the shadow that emerges inadvertently as a consequence of our development toward freedom and fullness.

With this frame, we can view Jesus' journey in the wilderness and his subsequent ministry with new eyes. The time in the desert was both a time of *purgation* and of *illumination*. The *purgation* is evident from his fasting—body, mind, soul and spirit—and from the temptations he encountered. There can be no doubt that this was a time in which Jesus moved to CLEAN UP. The *illumination* is evident from his emergence after "Jesus returned to Galilee in the power of the Spirit," and in one of his first sermons, quoting the scripture "the Spirit of the Lord is upon me," before declaring that scripture fulfilled in the sight of his listeners. Considering that the writers of the Gospels only mention the temptations encountered at the end of Jesus' fast, it's reasonable to consider that Jesus experienced and stabilized increasingly deep *states* of consciousness, and in the process wrestled with transcending the entirety of self he knew himself to be (ego, soul, Self, suchness) and including the entirety of the new self he was coming into. That, after tempting Jesus, the devil "left him until an opportune time," calls to mind our own perpetual experience with the ego! "The Witness is the last stand of the ego," were the words of Ken Wilber's teacher, just prior to his awakening. A semetic man at the dawn of the common era might very well have experienced these struggles as though they took place against an exterior opponent; and the writers of the Gospels might readily have described them that way.

This is not in any way to deny the reality of evil, which we see so evidently in the world today, whether in the genocide of the Uighurs, the mass killing of protestors in Myanmar, or for that matter, the U.S. Capitol riot. We simply want to note that many of the stories of the Bible, especially as they involved externalized forces of evil, can be seen in the light of modernity as internalized, and in some cases, the expected (though no less catastrophic) consequences of development and its inadvertent formation of shadow.

Three Dark Nights

While Evelyn Underhill discerned a significant dark night between the illumination and union stages of the states that she researched, subsequent research has found a dark night at the edge of each of the great states as they are stabilized. At the outer boundary of the gross (waking) state is the dark night of the senses; at the outer boundary of the subtle (dream) state, the dark night of the soul, and at the outer boundary of the causal (deep sleep) state, prior to nondual, is the dark night of the Self. These dark nights are encountered as the familiarity and the very identity of the earlier state no longer comforts the self, while the deeper state has not yet become the self's vantage point; it's experienced quite literally as a night between the evening of the earlier state and the dawning of the later one. As Wilber has noted, we are vulnerable at precisely these switch-points, and precisely through these dark nights, as part but not all of us are ready to make the jump of transcending and including.

The particular forms the temptations that the gospels describe are of note, foreshadowing the dark night of the Self that Jesus was destined for. In the first, Jesus, having eaten no food at all for 40 days, is tempted to turn stones into bread; in this way he is tested in body/heart and navigates the dark night of the senses. He replies with scripture: "one shall not live on bread alone." He is then tempted with power to rule over all the kingdoms of the world: surely an alternative path to becoming the Messiah than he had contemplated, in convening the kingdom of heaven. Here he is tempted in soul, passing through the dark night of the soul. He replies again with scripture: "Worship the Lord your God, and serve only God." The devil, getting wise to Jesus' command of scripture, takes him to the pinnacle of the Temple and tempts him on exactly that front: "if you are the son of God, throw yourself down from here, for it is written 'he will command the angels concerning you, to protect you…on their hands they will bear you up, so that you will not dash your foot against a stone.'" In this, Jesus is tempted in mind, and ventures into the dark night of the Self. He replies once more with scripture: "you shall not put the Lord your God to the test."

This sublime temptation is repeated in the moments prior to his death: as the Son, he's taunted to draw on the power of the Father to save himself; his reply is given in the words of the Twenty-Second Psalm, of complete confidence in love, against all odds and every probability. The three temptations thus symbolize the three dark nights in Jesus' journey through deepening states. We see his *purification*, his kenosis, a radically emptying of ego, soul and Self, and an emergent *illumination* that set the stage for his mission of fearless and ferocious love for all beings.

We noted that Jesus' fast in the desert is the forerunner to the great season of Lent, the 40-day fast that precedes the commemoration of Jesus' death and resurrection. The theme of Lent is to repent, from the Latin *paenitere*, defined as "to feel or express sincere regret or remorse about one's wrongdoing or sin." But perhaps much more helpful is the original Greek verb for this theme: *metanoia*, or change of consciousness. John the Baptist preached metanoia as the forerunner, and Jesus himself preached metanoia as he began his ministry. The theme of the wilderness is metanoia, and led by the Spirit, Jesus himself "put on the mind of Christ" that was so definitive in its knowing and loving through his mission to come.

A Burning Thought

As Jesus emerges from the desert—having faced the darkness within himself and having overcome it unto illumination of his states and stages—he now inhabits a profound new vantage point of states and a panoramic view from stages—much like the high mountain and pinnacle of the Temple from which the devil had just tempted him. Now he begins to face the darkness in others.

We saw that Jesus, in his movement beyond the highest stage that had been stabilized in his day, entered a trackless land into which few had ventured, and blazed his own trail there, with his signature virtue of love. We saw as well that individuals who progress to these (now) 3rd-tier stages exhibit the "superhuman capacities" that Wilber notes in *The Religion of Tomorrow*.

On numerous occasions Jesus "cast out" demons; while possession is a real phenomenon, in many cases the physical and psychological infirmities of Jesus' day can be explained and alleviated by modern science. But there were twenty-two recorded healings in the synoptic Gospels; these merit a closer look. Rather than taking our own critical worldview as "given,"

our best move forward is to consider the mindset from
which he was acting, consider the lenses with which
we're viewing, and consider the methodology by which
we can best understand these events. In the words of
Gibran:

> There are no miracles beyond the seasons,
> yet you and I do not know all the seasons. And
> what if a season shall be made manifest in the
> shape of a man?
>
> In Jesus the elements of our bodies and our
> dreams came together according to law. All
> that was timeless before Him became timeful
> in Him.
>
> They say He gave sight to the blind and
> walking to the paralyzed and that He drove
> devils out of madmen.
>
> Perchance blindness is but a dark thought
> that can be overcome by a burning thought.
> Perchance a withered limb is but idleness that
> can be quickened by energy. And perhaps the
> devils, these restless elements in our life, are
> driven out by the angels of peace and serenity.[1]

In Wilber's 20 tenets, the lower sets the possibilities of the higher, and the higher sets the probabilities
of the lower. When he descended the mountain after
the Sermon on the Mount, a man with leprosy came

and knelt before him and said "Lord, if you are willing, you can make me clean," and Jesus reached out his hand, touched him and replied "I am willing. Be clean!" And he was healed. In the midst of the kingdom that Jesus realized, countless possibilities became probabilities and then realities; countless promises were fulfilled. And even at the great boundary of death, he whose Awareness and consciousness raised his own crucified body, could surely raise the life of another. In Boulding's First Law: anything that exists is possible.

Agony in the Garden

The temptations in the wilderness are bookended by the agony in the garden. Here Jesus confronts his shadow for one last time. "Abba, Father, for you all things are possible; remove this cup from me; yet, not what I want, but what you want." We might frame Jesus' mind in terms of aversion of a higher state; Jesus has stabilized his *illumination* but not yet his complete *union*, and between the two there lies the dark night of the Self.

The dark night of the Self helps us to understand Jesus' distress and agitation. He is quite beyond the dark night of the senses—he is not afraid to die; in fact, he is consciously marching toward his death, and has shared that knowledge with his disciples. He has bid them farewell. He is beyond the dark night of the soul—he understands himself to be the Messiah, and has rejected every other path to convening the kingdom than the one he has chosen. His agitation is that of the dark night of the Self: he has understood his mission to embody the Torah, embody the Temple, embody the Messiah: embody God. He has taken matters into his own hands. He has accepted his mission without turning away; but in this dark night, there is no one to comfort him. He knows that despite the best of his understanding (his view, from his vantage point), in its very audaciousness, he could be catastrophically mistaken.

Here we see Jesus in his full humanity. He speaks the words "thy will be done," reminiscent of the words he gave his disciples when he taught them to pray. But as we saw, "thy kingdom come" does not, for Jesus, refer to a future time, or the end times; "thy will be done" is *now*. And "on earth, as it is in heaven" is *here*, the outer a perfect reflection of the inner, and "emptiness, not other than form, and form, not other than emptiness." He is approaching the divine, quite literally, with Leonard Cohen's request: "dance me to the end of love."

Five Original Sins

One more observation can be made around shadow, particularly in the state and stage that Jesus found himself in, emerging from the wilderness. What appears as the gateway to Awakened Awareness to those who approach it must seem too as a falling away as Spirit first pours itself into manifestation, if only in divine play. "The Fall" actually did take place through the great involutionary arc that culminated in the Big Bang. And if, in a lovely Orthodox Christian way of seeing it, sin is a forgetting of our being united to the Father, our Original Sin was the misidentification of consciousness with the external forms it was bound up in, rather than with the Awareness which animated that consciousness, in the form of a mind and a body. We are, in the impossibly deep voice of Leonard Cohen, the solitude of longing, and the love there confined; we are troubled dust, in which is concealed an undivided love.

Ken Wilber, with typical wit, entitled a teaching

of his: "Five Reasons You're Not Enlightened"; to the extent that Jesus came into the highest state and stage that had evolved in his time, we could examine the five reasons he *was* enlightened. And crucially, those five reasons can be seen as shadow, as aversion or allergy to a higher stage that we move into proximity to, and, from the vantage point of the higher state, five versions of Original Sin. Piercing through and moving beyond these emergent shadows is the culmination of evolution, in our case, drawn by Christ the Omega, who first realized the suchness on the other side, and draws all beings to Herself.

The first Original Sin—and therefore one of the final "allergies" that Jesus overcame—is conceptualization, or dualism; Madhyamika Buddhism points out this "falling away" and charts the return to the unqualifiable. We see Jesus' rebuke of the Pharisees as emblematic of this approach. Time and time again he was approached with elaborate stories ("a woman marries a man with seven brothers; he dies and she subsequently marries his brother, who also dies, and so on through the seven... with whom shall she be in heaven with?") to test him, and he replied "you do not know the scriptures nor the power of God. He is not the God of the dead, but the God of the living, for to him all are alive," to which no one dared to question him further. We see in Matthew Jesus' disdain for the "wise and learned" of his day, who had conceptualized God: God who was unknowable except in the loving consciousness of Christ:

> At that time Jesus said, "I praise you, Father, Lord of heaven and earth, because you have hidden these things from the wise and learned, and revealed them to little children. Yes, Father, for this is what you were pleased to do.
> "All things have been committed to me by my Father. No one knows the Son except the Father, and no one knows the Father except the Son and those to whom the Son chooses to reveal him." (Matthew 11:25-27)

The second Original Sin is objectification and separation; Yogachara and the Tantric paths are exemplary at overcoming this dualism. Jesus beautifully moved beyond this dualism in his transpersonal understanding and teaching. In the parable of judgement day, Jesus says that whatsoever you do to the least of my sisters, my brothers, that you do unto me. The least of his brothers and sisters were no longer objects, but the subjects of the love, or lack, from those to be judged, and Jesus saw in them and knew them to be one with his divine self, as Christ.

Jesus holds the sword of Manjushri time and time again, in cutting through this dualism, in his closing of the Sermon on the Mount:

> You have heard that it was said, "You shall love your neighbor and hate your enemy." But I say to you, "Love your enemies and pray for those who persecute you, so that you may be children of your Father in heaven; for *he makes his sun rise on the evil and on the good, and sends rain on the righteous and on the unrighteous.* For if you love those who love you, what reward do you have? Do not even the tax collectors do the same? And if you greet only your brothers and sisters, what more are you doing than others? Do not even the Gentiles do the same? Be perfect, therefore, as your heavenly Father is perfect." (Matthew 5:43-48)

His words—bridging dualism with love—are echoed in the farewell of Kahlil Gibran's *Prophet* to the people of Orphalese:

> But you do not see, nor do you hear, and it is well.
> The veil that clouds your eyes shall be lifted by the hands that wove it,

And the clay that fills your ears shall be pierced by those fingers that kneaded it.

And you shall see

And you shall hear.

Yet you shall not deplore having known blindness, nor regret having been deaf.

For in that day you shall know the hidden purposes in all things,

And *you shall bless darkness as you would bless light*.[2]

The third Original Sin is seeking, and being trapped in time: well understood and surpassed in the Dzogchen and Great Perfection traditions. We see Jesus, too, move across this territory in his final teachings to his apostles at the last supper. As they realize that his departure, though mysterious, is imminent, they begin to ask him increasingly insistent questions: when Jesus says "you know the way to the place that I am going" and Thomas says, "Lord, we do not know where you are going; how can we know the way?" Jesus replies "*I Am the way*"; when Philip asks, "show us the Father, and we will be satisfied," Jesus replies "*I Am in the Father, and the Father Is in me*." Jesus knew the truth of who he was, and recognized the seeking of his apostles, even as he knew his death to be imminent. His response reflects the Pathless Path and the truth that in the imminent consciousness of Christ, they beheld—always already—the transcendent consciousness of the Father, as Awareness itself.

The fourth Original Sin is differentiation and the mistaken identity that results. The Vedanta tradition is outstanding in overcoming this dualism. Every mind is supported by a body; the very form of mind, says Ramana Maharshi, is thought, and every "thought" arises with a corresponding "thing." So too, the very highest and first thoughts of Awareness itself. These thoughts, however lofty, arose with and became identified with things, and disidentified with the Awareness that was their source, their home, and in which they originated.

Jesus' words to his apostles at the Last Supper speak powerfully to his overcoming the "many-ness" that we perceive around us, and conceive ourselves to be a part of. His prayer repeats the realization he spoke to the Pharisees, "I and the Father are one," and extends that oneness to all who hear the good news of oneness:

> I pray also for those who will believe in me through their message, *that all of them may be*

one, Father, just as *you are in me and I am in you. May they also be in us so* that the world may believe that you have sent me. I have given them the glory that you gave me, *that they may be one as we are one— I in them and you in me*—so *that they may be brought to complete unity*. (John 17:20-23)

The fifth Original Sin is a lack of love. In this falling away, the love that was present in Awareness is forgotten as Awareness takes shape and comes into form. In fact, it is the love in Awareness that bridges the dualism and creates a path to non-dualism. This is clearly the path of Christ, and his commandment to love one another—where every other is loved as one's self, and every being is neighbor to every other—as he had loved them was indeed the "little way" he walked and pointed out.

The Darkness Yielding

I love to think of these five insights as five lanterns that light each of our ways, and illuminate the darkness of the thought that there ever was an other. The fifth lantern was the one that Jesus carried through the darkness of Gethsemane and into the darkness of the tomb. This lantern casts a stunning light amidst the others, and is beautifully entangled and entwined with them. Though Buddhist teacher Diane Musho Hamilton—in deference to the love that was of singular importance in Jesus' teaching—jokes that "in Buddhism, the closest thing to love is a vague sense of warmth," in fact the great sages who held the other lanterns also counsel love as the way beyond dualism. One can scarcely imagine a more tantric practice than Jesus, crucified, exchanging self and other as he breathed his last. In the Vajrayana Buddhist practice of tonglen, we breathe in suffering and breathe out compassion; with his dying breath, Jesus breathed in the suffering of all time and space and breathed out compassion as love to eternity, to infinity, a great last breath that we still feel upon our skin today.

Ramana Maharshi, in addressing the fourth Original Sin of differentiation, teaches that the heart is *hridayam*, the source (literally, the birth-place) of the mind; keeping the mind in the heart is called Self-wardness (*ahanmukham*), and when the mind thus abides in the heart, the "I" will vanish and the ever-existing "I-I", the Self alone, will shine. To be still as such is called "seeing through the eye of knowledge" (*jnana-drishti*) and gives fathomless meaning to the Psalm "be still and know that I Am God."

Contemporary Advaita Vedanta sage Sri Nisarga-datta Maharaj counsels his students to come into another mind (the mind of Christ, by any other name):

> ...which unites and harmonizes, which sees the whole in the part and the part as totally related to the whole...in going beyond beyond the limiting, dividing and opposing mind. In ending the mental process as we know it. When this comes to an end, that mind is born... It becomes rather a question of *love* seeking expression and meeting with obstacles. The inclusive mind is *love in action*, battling against circumstances, initially frustrated, ultimately victorious.[3]

When his student asks, between the spirit and the body, whether it is love that is the bridge, he responds

> What else? Mind creates the abyss, the heart crosses it.[4]

That love would be a great gateway to the endpoint of the Way is moving, and not surprising. Ken Wilber, in a set of sublime insights, has recently written of the feeling associated with the two permanent states beyond the three (waking, dreaming, deep sleep) which come and go: *turiya* (the fourth state) and *turiyatita* (beyond the fourth state). Turiya—the radical freedom of the Witness—says Wilber, invokes and evokes the feeling of Bliss (capitalized, to emphasize that it's quite beyond the bliss that we might ordinarily experience, with its opposite or misery). But there is one step further: turiyatita—the radical fullness of One Taste. In the movement from turiya to turiyatita, says Wilber, the "freedom from" the entire world becomes "one with" the entire world. And the feeling of the radical fullness of One Taste is Love.

When Christ says "I Am the Alpha, and I Am the Omega," the sense has always been that Christ, who is Love itself, is the first and the last. But now we can paint the picture, ever more vividly. "The Alpha" implies that on the involutionary jump, Spirit dives through a vast realm of possibility, and that the luminous Emptiness and darkness of that realm is pregnant with Love, as the Word. Indeed, we hear of this truth in the Prologue to the Gospel of John:

> In the beginning was the Word, and the Word was with God, and the Word was God. He was in the beginning with God. *All things came into being through him, and without him not one thing came into being.* (John 1:1-3)

And on the evolutionary return to the starting

point, from which Spirit will dive again, the last realm of form, the gateway between the Witness and One Taste is the Omega, which is Love. Love sends and blesses Spirit on its dive into form, and Love draws and welcomes form on its return to Spirit. Jesus the man embodied Christ and thus embodied Love, and moved in Love with every step. Greater Love has no one than to lay down one's life for their friends; Jesus considered all beings as friends, and laid down his life for them all.

In Christ, light from Light, we know a breakthrough—the footprints of Jesus up the mountain and the little way of love that leads to its summit, through shadows that obscure the oneness of the vantage point at the peak. But look closely, and you shall also see the lanterns of the East—dispelling the darkness—and illuminating the Great Way that also leads there. And be ever grateful for the light that they shine upon all of our paths, that we too might be light from Light, and awareness to Awareness itself.

FOUR
THE LINE IN THE SAND

It was a dark and stormy night. Darkness had fallen across the land at the ninth hour; the life of Jesus had ended in the mythic practice the Romans knew how to do to make an example of troublemakers: asphyxiation and exhaustion by crucifixion, as the condemned, after fighting for hours, can no longer support their lungs, can no longer breathe. His apostles had fled, for fear of the same fate. John has it that only Mary his mother, Mary of Magdala and "the disciple whom Jesus loved" remained at the cross; perhaps his sorrow was greater still, that his mother, his beloved and his best friend witnessed his suffering unto death.

The Turning of the Tables

I sometimes sadly smile in discussions with friends who claim that Jesus never existed. This is almost invariably a category error, in which today's methods are applied with no regard to the fact that the world was different at the dawn of the common era—not to mention that each of us inhabit a different *worldspace*, and there is no given *world*. One can read the beginning of the Gospel of Luke, for instance, and claim that no such decree went out from the Emperor Augustus that all the world should be registered! This sort of argument misses the point. History was different in those days and looked nothing like it does now, and Luke was attempting to ground a story which is virtually inexplicable in any case.

The fact of the matter is that Jesus writ love, and writ it large on the canvas of history, in ways we are still unpacking today. The Catholic catechism states that "no new public revelation is to be expected before the glorious manifestation of our Lord Jesus Christ" (!) but if so, then we have a great deal of unpacking still to do around the question, "who do we say that Christ is?" There is a reason we're still talking about turning the tables; there's a reason we're still talking about a line in the sand. He was fearless and he moved with no hesitation; *had he hesitated, the first stone would have been cast*. There's a reason that we can modestly claim, at the very least, that Jesus impacted the Western world up until this day, and that he's one of a handful of people that we name from the dawn of the common era (and many of the others we can name because of his impact on them). My contention is that his impact is quite beyond that, for reasons I described in *Fully Human*. He is among those who took Spirit's dive and, on the return, found a blank canvas, a breathtaking *vantage point* and a stunning *view* beyond, and held a vajra brush and all the colors in hand. Some of the beauty of love that we know today was painted as such by Jesus, who found Christ, and Christ, who found Jesus—and who so thoroughly knew and loved one another that there was no other, so much so that we call them one Person with two natures now. Of all men, Jesus was the man who demonstrated, in every word and every deed, how to SHOW UP.

Jesus had awakened to the nondual state, as witnessed in those words and his deeds; for his time, Jesus came into the highest stage unfolded to that time. He was enlightened in every way that one could be in his day, and therefore was at Ken Wilber's nondual Supermind. His was an aperture through which the light of Spirit poured directly into evolution, creating an incredibly powerful a d profound unfolding in his individual interior, and moving in the adjacent quadrants powerfully too. Jes s' expression of *awareness in his body*—what spiritu l teacher David Deida called "the measure of a man"—changed the course of history, in the turning of the ables and the line in the sand. And the kingdom of he ven that he realized within was not only a kingdom o "I," it was a kingdom of "we"; he told many followe s that "the kingdom had come very close" to them, a d that "the kingdom was in their midst." The kingd m of heaven is a subtle sangha that spans the centuri s and covers the earth; it is realized at a point outside of space and in a moment outside of time.

From Integr l theory we know that, for any holon to remain in existence, it must not only be enacted; it must be *etra-enacted*, and it must necessarily *tetra-mesh*—that s, it must be supported by its individual interior, i dividual exterior, collective interior, and collective ex erior elements. It must be supported by its junior olons. Should it fail on any of these necessary condit ons, it will be destroyed, according to Wilber's *twe y tenets*, the minimum set of conditions necessary to get a universe going. (I'm inclined to agree with Wilber on this point.) Integral theory further tells us that particularly strong ideas become so precisely due to their effective tetra-meshing. For instance, communism was a particularly potent idea that linked the means of production with the classes of society; that it went so terribly wrong can also be explained by Integral theory.

We can see the impact of Jesus through precisely these lenses: the waves that he made can be felt in all four quadrants. By all accounts he had a deep practice and had profoundly witnessed the second face of God by the time of his baptism. That he (or in John's Gospel, the baptist himself) heard the Father and saw the Spirit descend and remain on him is the best explanation of the writers of the time to describe a profound state experience, like Moses encountering Spirit in 1st-person (I Am who Am) and experiencing that Spirit in a burning bush outside of himself.

This deeply stabilized state of consciousness in Jesus—the kingdom of heaven—in the interior of his individual, began to have profound effects in the adjacent quadrants. We see Jesus moving definitively from the miracle of his "I" to build a miracle called "we," moving his profound 1st-person revelation into a

2nd-person community to realize the kingdom of heaven, and to enact the new earth. After praying through the night, he chooses his apostles; he astounds Nathanial (in whom there was "no deceit") by saying he saw him beneath the fig tree (though they'd never met, the fig tree was a sign of the coming Messiah, or anointed and promised one, and there is some secret about the fig tree, known to Nathaniel, and known by *gnosis* in Jesus). These events all take place in the *first chapter* of the Gospel of John, which began with "the Word became flesh." At this point in the gospel, the story of the incarnation (and the tetra-enaction of Spirit-in-evolution) has barely begun.

We also see Jesus moving his 1st-person revelation into decisive 3rd-person action: Chapter 2 begins with the first miracle of water into wine. He has somehow gained mastery over 3rd-person realities; they are called miracles because they are counter to the laws of nature (which, as we saw, are simply Kosmic habits). But for Jesus, they're quite simply faithful reflections, in the exterior world, of his interior state: enactions of the kingdom. The fact that he has stabilized his 1st-person state means that the 3rd-person reality holds, and the holon—however sublime seeming "water into wine"—is tetra-enacted. But Jesus, at this point, is hell-bent for Jerusalem, and in his beginning is his end.

Though one's interior-individual *intention* can influence both their interior-collective *culture* and their exterior-individual *behavior*, it's another matter altogether to influence one's exterior-collective *social* systems. But here we see Jesus having a massive effect as well in that domain, from its proximity to the culture that Jesus inspired and the singular impact his actions had on the systems that followed his life. Jesus directly spoke about social systems on certain occasions. The famous text "For where two or three are gathered in my name, I am there among them" was actually given in the context of establishing a system for resolving disputes. His many statements about the kingdom of heaven and the kingdom of God evoke a utopia that he has in heart and mind, in the interior and exterior quadrants alike, and have inspired social and political systems throughout history.

The United States Constitution, a unique document at its time due to its rational, post-ethnocentric character—"we hold these truths to be self-evident..."—was inspired by the teachings of Jesus and their effects on the framers. It can be critiqued on its lack of efficacy two and a half centuries later—that all "men" are created equal neglected women, not to mention the slaves and their descendants—but the great reformers like Harriet Tubman, Rosa Parks and the Reverend Martin Luther King were all directly inspired by Jesus, and sought their reforms informed by his teaching. King studied under Mahatma Gandhi—who transmitted to him Jesus' teaching to turn the other cheek—before proclaiming "let freedom ring!" in the shadow of the Lincoln Memorial, and the light of Jesus' "he has sent me to proclaim freedom for the prisoners," the words fulfilled in the synagogue at Nazareth two millennia earlier.

The monumental benefit of our twenty centuries' distance from Jesus of Nazareth—and Christ in History—is the vantage point that we can take, and the view we can behold. As Gibran wrote:

> When you part from your friend, you grieve
> not; For that which you love most in him may
> be clearer in his absence, as the mountain to
> the climber is clearer from the plain.[1]

Jesus himself reiterated this to his apostles, in his farewell, saying:

> I still have many things to say to you, but you cannot bear them now, and... but because I have said these things to you, sorrow has filled your hearts. Nevertheless I tell you the truth: it is to your advantage that I go away, for if I do not go away, the Spirit will not come to you; but if I go, I will send the Spirit to you. (John 16:12, John 16:7)

From our 20th century view, and the vantage point of the holy ground we stand on, we can hardly speculate on his knowledge of his identification with the Second Person of the Trinity; these were later projections onto the inexplicable miracle of the man who was God, the God who was man: words to describe the indescribable. But we know that he knew the Torah quite literally by heart, that he loved the Temple, that he lived in hope of the coming of Israel's God and the anointed, the chosen, the Messiah. But for Jesus, it was more than that—at his baptism, we hear from the heavens that he *is* "the chosen." There must have been a moment—perhaps in Spirit's great dive in which Christ would meet humanity—in which Jesus, echoed with Isaiah:

> I saw the Lord sitting on a throne, high and lofty; and the hem of his robe filled the temple.

And [the seraphs] called to another and said:

"Holy, holy, holy is the Lord of hosts; the whole earth is full of his glory." The pivots on the thresholds shook at the voices of those who called, and the house filled with smoke. Then I heard the voice of the Lord saying, "Whom shall I send, and who will go for us?" And I said, "Here am I; send me!" (Isaiah 6:1-4,8)

"Here am I; send me!" And he who said "here am I" became "I am." And set out not to follow the Torah, but to be the *Torah-giver*; not to worship in the Temple but to *embody* it, to tabernacle with us; not to wait for the promise but to *fulfill* it, in the most Sacred Heart of his shattered body, in the broken-open clarity of his mirror-mind. If time is seen as a holarchy, the previous moments (the Law and the Prophets, what the second Temple meant to Israel, and how she longed for God's return) were the junior holon which set the *possibility* for the life of Jesus in his present moment. The completeness of his kenosis in that present moment set the *probability* that these would all be fulfilled. And the nature of Love itself saw to the certainty, in the Emptiness of the tomb.

On the Turning Away

What if God was one of us? Ken Wilber writes beautifully on the practitioner at Supermind: having stabilized the nondual state and the highest stage to have unfolded in human history to date, at one with them all. In even that practitioner there can be shadow; even there, one can turn away: shadow at Supermind:

> To contract at all in the face of this undivided wholeness awareness, this total painting of all that is existing in this timeless all-inclusive present, is to set in motion the self-contraction, the separate self-sense that latches onto the relative, finite, conventional small self—a necessary functional entity for this manifest world created by the True Self itself, along with the rest of creation—but latches onto that small self, or "I", as if it were itself the True Self, or "I-I", thus setting in motion the entire train of events known as ignorance, illusion, Maya, deception, the fallen world, the world of the lie. This is transmitted in each and every lower structure present, and the radically enlightened nature of Supermind becomes lost and obscured in wave after wave of avoidance.

And that avoidance rests on this, what we might call "primordial avoidance"—the very first subtle looking away. If we go back to the single, indivisible, total painting notion, there is some element, no matter how small or seemingly insignificant, that for whatever reason I don't want to look at, to be aware of, to notice, to allow into my awareness—that single, primary turning away, looking away, moving away. That primordial avoidance sets in motion the events that are, at this level, the dominant cause of the world of Maya, illusion, ignorance, deception. And every level, top to bottom, is infected with this delusion."[1]

Of course, God's thoughts are above our thoughts, God's ways above our ways. But we saw Jesus go into the wilderness for forty days and come out of the wilderness with the notion of fulfilling the Torah, rebuilding the Temple and moving in himself to make the promise of God be realized. Jesus emerged from the wilderness as I Am who Am. If we can understand his thoughts, perhaps we can shed some light on God's thoughts....

One of the pithy answers to the question "why is there something rather than nothing?" is that "it's no fun having dinner alone." Spirit creating form—simply by imagining it—is Spirit's play. If Love emerged as the emotion of *turiyatita*—the highest state, in which the Witness merges with the witnessed, then that Love needed a home here, and Love found its home in the great bridge between dust and Divinity: the human heart.

Father Thomas convened the Snowmass Dialogues in the 1970's; for 40 years they were a sublime set of gatherings between leaders and then deeply friends from the world's spiritual traditions. In his farewell remarks to his old friends, he said: "God is playing an exquisite game of hide-and-seek with us. And playing so well, in fact, that the Buddhists still haven't found her!" Such was the humor of Father Thomas, and the wisdom as well. Spirit got lost for the joy of being found, and Love was created that the heart could cross the abyss of the mind, to follow Spirit's footsteps back through consciousness to Awareness, from which she burst forth.

We can only see Spirit's involution from this side, where there is a gate in Spirit's first stepping down into states. We see a oneness become a twoness, and a whole become an inside with an outside. We see the fall, and we look for an original sin. We see that Spirit has turned away, but perhaps it's simply Spirit at play. And, per Wilber—due to evolution, the novel emergent, and *our hand* in painting the canvas—the product of our evolutionary return through stages is unknown, *even to Spirit*. "As for the future," wrote Antoine de St-Exupery, "your task is not to predict it, but rather to enable it.'[3]

But if manifestation is Spirit's play, why is there suffering? In his penultimate moment of love—as Jesus breathes his last—it is sometimes said that, in the pain of searing loss, "the Father turned his Face away." But Jesus the man never turned away.

Jesus is the Bodhisattva of Love. A bodhisattva (one whose being is enlightened) promises to attain (or in some translations, postpone for others' benefit) enlightenment so as to help all beings along the way to that enlightenment. His attainment was of an awakening to, illumination by, and union with God. But that attainment was never for himself—in fact, he emptied himself—and he ever launched himself into the midst, the very heart of suffering. Or rather he stood timelessly still, in the stillness of "be still and know that I Am God," and life, which is suffering, came to him. But this noble teacher too spoke four Noble Truths:

of life as suffering ("I am thirsty"), of the origin of that suffering ("though he was in the form of God, Jesus did not deem equality with God something to be grasped at; rather he emptied himself....") and its cessation ("come to me, all you who labor and are heavily burdened, and I will give you rest"). And he himself was the way leading to the cessation of suffering.

The Broken Heart Above

Jesus, we have seen, knew the scriptures well and increasingly moved to bring them to fulfillment in himself, before one iota would pass away. We saw that he lived *fully divine*, on his spiritual way, until he himself became the way; from there he took his vantage point. We saw that he lived *fully human*, bursting through the mythic of his day, into a trackless land in which he blazed a trail of love; from there he took his view. He stared into shadow in the desert, and in the garden, keeping vigil through each of the dark nights, and freeing his life force to inhabit the highest vantage point, to behold the most all-embracing view possible. When one is at evolution's edge—as Jesus was—Spirit pours into form in a relatively unadulterated way. The possibilities are captivating, the probabilities are enchanting, and the impact of one person can be history-changing.

Thus Jesus was not only a Torah teacher; he was a Torah *giver*. He knew its lines and sought to fulfill them with his every movement. His ministry began with a reading from Isaiah "the Spirit of the Lord is upon me" that was fulfilled in his listeners' hearing. Incredibly, on the cross, when seemingly even "the Father turned his face away," Jesus nonetheless quoted the words of the Twenty-Second Psalm, and *they are fulfilled in real time.*

> My God, my God, why hast thou forsaken me?
>
> Why art thou so far from helping me, from the words of my groaning?
>
> O my God, I cry by day, but thou dost not answer; and by night, but find no rest.
>
> Yet thou art holy, enthroned on the praises of Israel.
>
> But I am a worm, and no man; scorned by men, and despised by the people.
>
> All who see me mock at me,
>
> they make mouths at me, they wag their heads;
>
> a company of evildoers encircle me; they have pierced my hands and feet—
>
> I can count all my bones—they stare and

gloat over me;
    they divide my garments among them,
    and for my raiment they cast lots.
    (Psalm 22:1-3,6-7, 17-18)

The psalm ends with great hope, but Jesus did not have the opportunity to finish it. Nonetheless, we see in Jesus not only Cohen's "troubled dust," but especially his "undivided love." And we see this abandoned man teaching love from his most Sacred Heart below to God's broken Heart above.

Exchanging Self and Other

In the stillness of the chapel at Snowmass, I listened intently to the Good Friday Gospel. In John, the evangelist often refers to "the disciple whom Jesus loved." It is this disciple who, when Jesus foretells that one of his apostles will betray him, leans his head on Jesus' heart and asks "Lord, who is it?" It is this disciple who outruns Peter to Jesus' tomb when Mary of Magdala, after going to anoint the body of Jesus early on the third day following his death, returns and announces "they have taken the Lord from the tomb." This disciple is never named, perhaps to invite us to walk a mile in his sandals: *you and I are the disciple whom Jesus loved*. I sought to be in that disciple's sandals at the foot of Jesus' cross, with Mary his mother and Mary of Magdala.

The words of the Twenty-Second Psalm, though unspoken were perfectly fulfilled:

> For he has not despised or abhorred
> he affliction of the afflicted;
> and he has not hid his face from him,
> but has heard, when he cried to him.
> (Psalm 22:24)

Upon the cross, he breathed in the *suffering*—not just his own but the suffering of all beings ever to suffer—and he breathed out *compassion*, as Zechariah, the father of John the Forerunner had foretold: "in the tender *compassion* of our God, the dawn from on high shall break upon us." And then, as though in the sublime Buddhist practice of tonglen—exchanging self and other—Jesus breathed his last.

The Tomb was Empty

The Tulkus are said to leave messages indicating where they will be reborn (though of reincarnation, Shankara, the great teacher of Advaita Vedanta, taught "verily, there is no other transmigrant but the

Lord."). In the Mystery of mysteries, Awareness, in the consciousness of Christ, was resurrected in the mind and body of Jesus, the very man who had been crucified and had died, three days before. He died with such love on the cross—breathing in the suffering of embodiment and breathing out the compassion of I Am who Am—that the love he cultivated through awakening, purgation, illumination—that love too—entered its dark night. That love too was crucified and entombed. That love remained with him, homeless after his Sacred Heart beat for the last time; that love, a refugee, with no place to go, apart from the one who tabernacled among us, and whose destroyed body lay wrapped in a linen cloth. With his emptying, his *kenosis* of body, mind, soul and Spirit, Jesus *forced God's hand* and left love no choice but to raise that body so that it could become the Temple. So badly broken was his body, so shattered his Sacred Heart, so thoroughly unfulfilled the scriptures, and utterly unrealized the promise, that Love lifted him from *savasana*, as Love lifts us all. So radically Empty was the tomb, and the *turiya* he reposed in, that Love knelt down to lift his footsteps in *turiyatita*, to which Love is the gateway, where Alpha is Omega and flesh becomes Word.

Awareness, Christ Consciousness and the mind and body of Jesus are perfectly in union, perfectly wed in a person who is fully human, fully divine. The Spirit of the Lord is upon the Bodhisattva of Love. In his most Sacred Heart, the kingdom of heaven—the nondual state-stage of consciousness—is in our midst. And in response to the question of the old hymn *Down to the River to Pray*, "who shall wear the starry crown?" the Mind of Christ is held at the very crown of each of our own weary heads.

He was seen first by Mary of Magdala—the apostle to the apostles—then Peter and John, who, too experienced the Emptiness of the tomb. And he was seen by the others; Thomas put his finger in the hand that had been pierced, and his hand in the side that had been lanced. Each, though scattered at his death, was willing to die in the testimony of his Aliveness. When they encountered him, he was different—but so were they; it was on that different ground that they met, and from a vantage point never before taken came a view never before seen. It was holy ground, and each removed their sandals. And in his bare feet he still walks across the uncharted waters, and in our slumber, treads gently on our trackless shores, whispering to us to Awaken.

From Integral, we know that everyone is right; though some are more right than others. Regarding the resurrection, we consider how the magical in the story appeals to magical believers, how the mythic in the story gives a deep purpose to mythic believers, how the rational challenges us: "what if they found the bones?" and regards all the miracles—and particularly the Miracle of miracles—with the haunting words of George and Ira Gershwin: "It ain't necessarily so." The levels don't end there, of course, so again we ask from Integral, and from 3rd-tier. At each stage and from each state, the answer becomes more true, more good, more beautiful. Notice that Jesus did not appear to everyone, but only those who had "eyes to see, and ears to hear." Jesus took a vantage point and regarded a view, and at a certain Kosmic Address, there found Christ, and never turned away. His teaching was not to admire him on a wall, or to take him as an invisible, conversational friend. He taught by injunction: do as I have done (and greater things than these). If you want to know who Christ is, the Way is illuminated, the community of the adequate is multitude, and the retinue is profound.

If Jesus seems "larger than life" that's because, in discovering his Christhood, he quite literally is. He turned the tables in the Temple, but he also turned the tables of history, and illuminated the dark ages with the light of the only commandment he ever gave, quite simply to love. He drew a line in the sand, in the shadow of the Temple, but he also drew a line in the sands of time: before him, God was transcendent; in him, God is immanent. Before him, Herod and Pilate wrestled for the kingdom; in him, the kingdom was "not of this world," but nonetheless had come very close and was in fact in their midst. Before him, "an eye for an eye, a tooth for a tooth"; in him, "turn the other cheek." Before him, "the world is illusory"; in him, Brahman alone is real, and Brahman is the world. Before him, "life is suffering"; in him, there is a way out of suffering, and "I Am" the way.

The conclusion of the Sermon on the Mount ("Be perfect, as you heavenly Father is perfect") is scarcely believable and seemingly unattainable, but not only did Jesus carry out that injunction in his case—he showed himself to be the way. A helpful translation of that impossible commandment is this: "therefore set no bounds upon your love, just as God sets no bounds upon God's love." Love is boundless, and though we are bounded, love in its boundlessness pitched its tent with us, that by the mystery of the water and wine, we might share in love's divinity: this love, humbled, to share in our humanity.

> Come to me, all you who labor and are heavily burdened,
> And I will give you rest
> Take my yoke upon yourselves, and learn from me
> For I am meek and humble of heart
> And you will find rest for your souls
> Yes, my yoke is easy
> And my burden is light. (Matthew 11:28-30)

The Seven Words of Gibran

Love, take me.
Take me, Beauty.
Take me, Earth.
I take you,
Love, Earth, Beauty.
I take
God.

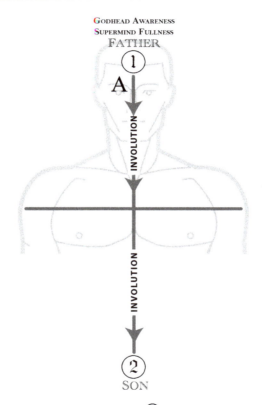

The Sign of the Cross begins from ① the forehead (the Alpha) to the solar plexus ② (crown chakra to solar plexus chakra) representing God's involution as the Son, the Word becoming flesh...

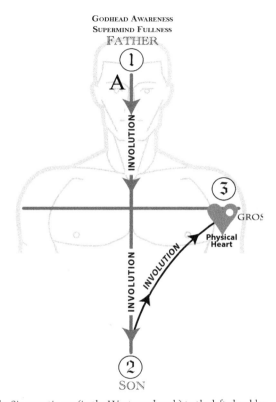

GODHEAD AWARENESS
SUPERMIND FULLNESS
FATHER
①
A
INVOLUTION
③
GROS
Physical
Heart
INVOLUTION
INVOLUTION
②
SON

The Sign continues (in the Western church) to the left shoulder, ③ close to our physical heart, as the Word "pitches His tent" and tabernacles among us. In the Eastern church, the more ancient Sign is made to the right shoulder first, emphasizing Theosis and Divinity coming through humanity...

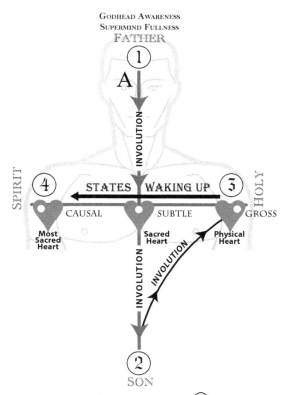

As we move our hand from our left shoulder ③ —across our physical heart, our sacred heart and our most sacred heart—to our right shoulder ④, I meditate on our awakening through the great states: embodying the gross, subtle, causal states and the nondual heart in which they arise...

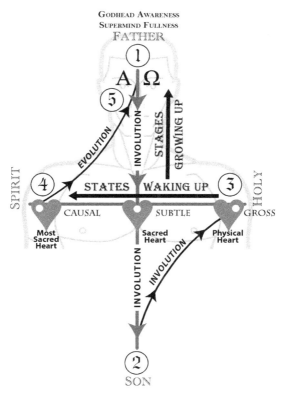

The Sign of the Cross traditionally ends there. An Integral Christian practice might return the hand to the crown chakra, honoring our evolution and growing up through stages of consciousness ⑤ where Christ has gone to prepare a place for us, and as Christ the Omega, draws us to Himself. "We shall be like Christ, for we shall see Him as He Is."

PART II

Christ In Mystery

FIVE

THE MOST SACRED HEART

Twenty centuries ago, the Man came around. He never strayed far from the dusty roads of Judea, and by drawing a line too far, he was condemned by the authorities of the day, secular and religious alike. He died on a hillside outside of the walls of Jerusalem, abandoned by humanity and, apparently, divinity. With his dying words he quoted the Twenty-Second Psalm, and forgave those who killed him. His apostles went on with their lives, even, as they supposed, Jesus had to go on with his death.

From the first apostles to the ancient Desert Mothers and Fathers, to the medieval mystics, to the renaissance theologians, to post-postmodern philosophers, many have deliberated on and proclaimed who they believed Jesus to be. The question for us now— and the only question—is who do *we* say that Christ is?

On the *Way of Embodied Love*, each of these terms are crucial and definitive. Among the women and men who've moved the world throughout history, and made history, Jesus' cardinal virtue was undoubtedly *love*. He summed up the Law and the Prophets with the commandment to "love the Lord your God with all your heart, all your mind, all your soul, and all your strength," and the second, like the first: "you shall love your neighbor as yourself." When he gave a new commandment, it was to "love one another as I have loved you."

But the love of Christ was irrelevant unless it landed and came through the mind and body of a human person. This realm was created for love, and duality itself was created for love. The love of Christ was *embodied* in Jesus, who showed by his words and definitively, by his deeds, what the love of a human life could do. Throughout his life and especially in his death, his choice was to make love the novel emergent in the new moment. He calmed the seas, but we are still feeling the power of the waves he awoke, simply by fearlessly loving in every moment. Christ was Divinity to dust, and Jesus, dust to Divinity. But having grounded his divinity, the Word pitched his tent with us; Christ's love ever touched the earth. Jesus gave sight to the man blind from birth by spitting on the ground and making mud to place on his eyes. It's hard to imagine a more visceral and embodied act of earthly love, than to make the earth itself the instrument of divine healing; that minor miracle was a holographically perfect symbol of the Miracle of miracles: the entire unfolding of Spirit's dive into Jesus of Nazareth. "Though he was in the form of God, Jesus did not deem equality with God something to be grasped at; rather, he emptied himself…and the Word became flesh, and pitched his tent among us." He knelt down and washed the feet of each of his apostles in the upper room, the night before he died; and doubtless, the feet of the Magdalen too.

The embodied love of Christ, in Jesus, is powerful. But *I say to you*: that is not why he came. It is our *awakening*, in the sight of Evelyn Underhill, but not yet our *illumination*; not yet our *union*. The message from Christ, and from history—Christ in evolution— could hardly be clearer: WAKE UP.

Kahlil Gibran, in voicing the perspective of "a man from Lebanon, nineteen centuries afterward," says of Jesus:

Master, Master Poet,
Master of our silent desires,
The heart of the world quivers with the throb-
bing of your heart,
But it burns not with your song.
The world sits listening to your voice in tran-
quil delight,
But it rises not from its seat
To scale the ridges of your hills.
Man would dream your dream but he would
not wake to your dawn
Which is his greater dream.
He would see with your vision,
But he would not drag his heavy feet to your
throne.[1]

Our illumination and union open to us when we
understand and embark upon the *Way*. When Jesus
answered Philip in his plea: "show us the way" and
Pilate in his question: "what is truth?" he answered
definitively: "*I Am* the way, the truth and the life." The
way, the truth and the life is the way of embodied love.
And the divine Christ, on the lips of the man Jesus,
said unmistakably, "I Am that."

We saw that Jesus' way, when looked at through
the remarkable modern lenses available to us, can be
seen in terms of his stabilizing ever-deepening *states*

of consciousness, culminating in the proclamation of his identity: "Before Abraham was, I Am", and progressing through the *stages* of consciousness that were available at the time, to GROW UP, culminating in a profound trans-mythic, transpersonal awareness: of the earth he said, in an eternal gesture, "this is my body." We also saw him CLEAN UP, wrestling with *shadow* in himself and others, liberating his life force to move him powerfully to the summit of those two journeys. The result was a human lifetime that was definitive in demonstrating what love could do, even beyond death. He of all people SHOWED UP in four quadrants, drawing *love* in the sand and painting it on the canvas, a form for the future that "descended, unadulterated," and poured into evolution as Spirit, directly in the image and likeness of God: a novel emergent whose effects are incalculable.

By walking a mile in his sandals—trying to understand what he might have been thinking, what he might have been feeling as he moved in Israel's midst, we can liberate him from the medieval Christologies projected onto him, even with the best of intentions, and can allow him to be fully human. And that in turn can liberate us to see that his journey in so many ways is not unlike our own—a deeply human journey which had sensed the outpouring of Spirit and sought to follow those footsteps back: body, mind, consciousness, Awareness, from dust to Divinity and back. So while, through twenty centuries, he can seem distant in time, these lenses allow us to see him in new ways, with implications that are earthshaking and groundbreaking for our own journeys. Jesus walked the way of embodied love, uniting humanity and divinity in his most Sacred Heart, unto Christ. And we too are invited to the way of embodied love, following in his footsteps, in our particular case.

The "good news" of emerging Integral awareness is that evolution happens, and it happens in four directions. Within me and within us, and outside of me and outside of us, Spirit is pouring into and as evolution. The deepening knowledge-as-love, *jnana-drishti* within me is supported by matter and energy that is progressively more intricate and subtle, as my very body. And since I know and am known by you, within yourself too it is deeply true, and within every human, and the community of all sentient beings, however far down you take that sentience: "consider the lilies."

On my Grandmother's night table there was a

picture of Jesus revealing his Sacred Heart. However much we might write off traditionalism from our modern and postmodern perspectives, there were precious truths in that image. The Sacred Heart was pictured in the center of Jesus' chest, not to the left where our gross hearts reside, but in the center, where our subtle hearts reside. Our gross hearts beat every second, pumping blood to every cell; by definition, when that heartbeat ceases, our embodiment has come to an end. Our subtle heart is where heaven and earth meet, and heaven and earth are entangled there as nowhere else. Abraham Joshua Heschel taught "The human is the knot in which heaven and earth are interlaced." Christ, embodied in Jesus, revealed his Sacred Heart, which went to eternity and infinity, even as his gross heart beat for the last time.

But there is a heart still more sacred, and a form yet more profound. In Meister Eckhart's sublime thought, prior to God was *Godhead*, and no less than the Trinity—Father, Son, and Holy Spirit—emerged from Godhead. The Son is the Word that the Father has spoken, and that Word emanated and echoed on the waves of the Spirit. In every moment of involution, evolution, God the Father, God the Mother, speak the Word: God the Daughter, God the Son. The Word is carried on the waves of the Spirit, divine parent to divine child (involution), and divine child to divine parent (evolution). The causal heart is the heart when the heart is first imagined, an idea in the mind of God that springs into archetypal form.

And if, as the great Hindu sage Shankara said, the number of transmigrants is one, then the *most* Sacred Heart of Christ—the causal heart, of which there is but one—is beating in us as well. The way that Jesus spoke to Philip was Christ, and the injunction was as Christ instructed: "do the things that I have done, and greater things than these, as I am going to the Father. And I will send the Spirit…." Christ, in a football analogy, "left it all on the field," including the most Sacred Heart. We find ourselves walking on the same field; on our embodied way of love, it is that heart that we find. That heart is ours to take up too.

The causal heart is a Word spoken by the transcendent God, and by speaking the Word, the transcendent is made immanent: the Word became flesh, and tabernacled among us. But even as Jesus was the Word—according to eminent theologian Raimon Pannikar—"we too are little words of God." Ram Dass points to the very first words that God speaks, and in their speaking, they become form; God asks Adam in the garden to name all the created beings, and by being named, they too come into being. The Word is an idea of God, and so are we; Meister Eckhart tells us that when the Trinity emerges from Godhead, *so too do we*. We share with God the very same, holy Ground: what Thomas Merton called "the hidden ground of love." So whether we emerge as descended from God the Father, God the Mother, or a sibling to Jesus our Brother, or as an emanation of the Spirit of evolution, we emerge with the Trinity, and we are invited to what Thomas Merton knew by gnosis as "the general dance." We are being danced to the end of Love. The most Sacred Heart of Christ is the causal heart; the number of transmigrants is one, and that heart beats within your breast, and within mine.

The sign of the cross beautifully traces the *involution* of Christ: "though he was in the form of God, Jesus did not deem equality with God something to be grasped at. Rather, he emptied himself...." We say "in the name of the Father, and of the Son" as we move our hand from our head down to the solar plexus to honor Spirit's involution among us, the Word becoming flesh. And then we move it to our gross heart, even as Christ took the form of Jesus the man. But completing the sign of the cross, it is we who are the *evolution*—gross heart to subtle heart to causal heart, through the states of consciousness that Jesus mastered. Our journey is to take this precious human birth, this precious human life, with its gross heart-beat, come into our subtle heart with all the unique, irreplaceable beauty of its unfolding in the love of our lives, and be united in the causal, most Sacred Heart with Christ. In truth, we live these three mysteries in every moment, along the way of embodied love. Our nondual Christian practice is to live each of these deeply, simultaneously, as the nondual heart—which never enters the stream of time—and in which these hearts emerge, as waves upon the vast ocean of Love.

By the Mystery of this Water and Wine

At the penultimate moment of the Mass of our Lord's Supper, the priest pours a drop from a vial of water into a vial of wine. The gesture is made along with a prayer, though whispered: "by the mystery of this water and wine, may we come to share in the Divinity of Christ, who humbled Himself to share in our humanity." That is the essence of the Christian faith, though it is whispered softly and seldom heard.

To hear this prayer in all its depth, the only response is to fall to your knees. "To be spiritual," says Rabbi Heschel, "is to be amazed." You realize that, in truth, it is not a drop of wine being poured into a vial of water: that is, we are not commemorating the unique Saviour Jesus coming amongst the throngs of millions, then billions of lost souls. Rather, *it is a drop of water being poured into a vial of wine.* We as human beings—and all sentient beings—are being immersed in Divinity. And there is more: a wise connoisseur friend of mine pointed out that when a fine wine is not yet ready to drink, pouring in a drop of water opens the wine, so that in a moment, the flavor the vintner imbued and intended is fully released. By the mystery of this water and wine, we, in our emptiness, allow God to come into God's fullness, in the Spirit of evolution. Mary of Magdala came to the tomb, but it was *Empty*; she shared the good news with Peter and John, and they, too, found the tomb Empty. The great modern theologian Karl Rahner said that humanity is the mystery of infinite emptiness and God, the mystery of infinite fullness. Jesus knew that emptiness: "though he was in the form of God, not deeming equality with God something to be grasped at…but rather, he emptied himself," thus *forcing God's hand.* If nature abhors a vacuum, how much more so does Divinity abhor emptiness, with no move but to fill it with the only substance that Divinity has—Divinity itself, but Divinity-as-humanity?

Father Thomas Keating was fond of saying that the entire purpose of the Christian tradition is to come into the same experience that Jesus had of the Father: as "Abba," literally, "Daddy." As imminent, intimate, closer to us, per Meister Eckhart, than we are to ourselves. The Christian tradition is to convene the kingdom of heaven; but that kingdom is within, here and now, as the most profound state of consciousness. The kingdom is indeed in our midst and has come very close to us, nearer than we are to ourselves.

Though Jesus' spoken teachings are prolific, his actions are a deeper teaching yet; his words are reflected and magnified, amplified in his deeds. He taught his followers to "follow" him, meaning do as he had done (and greater things than these). In that sense, the injunction was not so much to pray to him but to *pray as he prayed*. That means to approach God in each of God's three faces: that the words spoken in prayer were to be spoken *as* Spirit, *at* Spirit and *about* Spirit. In a nondual Christian practice—following Jesus' practice as known in the scriptures—we approach and then inhabit these faces, as the circumstances of our lives call for: from our moment-to-moment Awareness, residing in the consciousness of I Am, embodied in the precious human lives to which we bring our minds, and our hearts.

Practicing the three faces of God creates openings that we might not have known, had we approached only one of the faces. For example, the complete *kenosis* that we're moved to as we approach Spirit in 2nd-person can open us to inhabit I Amness—Spirit in 1st-person—in a much deeper way (this was likely Jesus' experience). The depth of the I Amness can then help us to see the world (Spirit in 3rd-person) as not other than ourselves, but in fact the perfect reflection of the kingdom realized within, and waves upon the waters of our infinite ocean of being.

I Am who Am

We saw Jesus, not long after emerging from his *illumination* in the wilderness, make a definitive statement, "Very truly, I tell you, before Abraham was, I Am." Here he is speaking as Spirit in 1ˢᵗ-person, through the first face of God. The tense he uses is important: he is not claiming to have come from a moment before Abraham; he is claiming to come from a moment outside of time. "I Am" is a singularly sublime statement, East and West.

Contemporary Advaita Vedanta Hindu sages have spoken magnificently on the practice of I Am. Ramana Maharshi gave a beautiful teaching in this regard in a precious, small booklet *Who Am I?*, and Sri Nisargadatta Maharaj speaks profoundly on the topic in *I Am That*. For both, I Am is a *via negativa* path that negates all that we are not (but think we are) to arrive at Spirit, and Spirit is known in love by *jnana-drishti* as *Satchitananda*: Being, Consciousness, Bliss. But it is also an injunctive path: Ramana Maharshi's point in this precious little book is to move us to begin on the path of self-inquiry, asking "who am I?" endlessly and knowing, when all else falls away, simply that "I Am." When a thought arises—any thought—you ask, "to whom did the thought arise?" The answer is "to me," and the final question arises again: "who am I?" Sri Nisargadatta Maharaj's dialogues point in the same direc-

tion: let your body abide in your mind; let your mind
abide in your consciousness; turn your consciousness
within, to Awareness, and abide in Awareness. Resting
in the Awareness of "I Am," you simply Are, and the
moment you become anything, if anything you become Being, Consciousness, Bliss. Maharaj knew the
Truth: *I Am That*.

In the reading of John's gospel, Jesus went to the
Mount of Olives, and early in the morning he came
down again to the Temple; the woman caught in adultery was brought before him and he definitively drew
the line in the sand. Later that day he responds to the
question "are you greater than our father Abraham?"
with his equally definitive words: "before Abraham
was, I Am." We can imagine his spending the night
praying on the Mount of Olives, as was his custom,
and descending from the mountain and into the world
and its suffering, to draw a line in the sand and to
speak the most definitive claim of his life. There was
power in his deeds and in his words, and the power
was sourced in his sense of I Amness. If we are to pray
as Jesus taught us, by his deeds, we too are invited to
sit as I Am who Am. The practice is the same, East and
West, since I Am is beyond form, and I Am in Jesus is

the same as I Am in Ramana, and I Am in Maharaj. And I Am who Am is within us, too.

The divine, said Heschel, "rings our hearts like a bell." When I am so awakened, a powerful practice for me is to lie in *savasana* (corpse pose, in yoga) and simply rest as I Am. I breathe twice deeply to acknowledge the knower and the known in the various readings of the name of Israel's God YHWH: "I Am who Am," "I Am That I am," before letting the knower and the known drop away—as merely attributes or ornaments of the knowing that they are—so that, at the third breath, all that remains is: "I Am." And remain as such, in *jnana-drishti*, consciousness holding mind and body, and abiding in Awareness. And there to remain until a line must be drawn in the sand, or kind words spoken in the embodied love I know I must bring.

In creating us, God asked a question; in awakening us, God answers the question. Thomas Merton writes:

> The life of contemplation implies two levels of awareness: first, awareness of the question, and second, awareness of the answer. Though these are two distinct and enormously different levels, yet they are in fact an awareness of the same

thing. The question is, itself, the answer. And we ourselves are both. But we cannot know this until we have moved into the second kind of awareness. We awaken, not to find an answer absolutely distinct from the question, but to realize that the question is its own answer. And all is summed up in one awareness – not a proposition, but an experience: 'I AM'.[2]

When practicing self-inquiry, teaches Ramana, the loving knowledge that remains is Being, Consciousness, Bliss. So too, in John's Gospel, there are seven words that Jesus uses, in the first emanation of I Am in his case. They are these:

"I Am the resurrection and the life," John 11:25; "I Am the light of the world," John 8:12; "I Am the good shepherd," John 10:11; "I Am the bread of life," John 6:35 "I Am the gate," John 10:9; "I Am the way, the truth, and the life," John 14:6; and "I Am the true vine," John 15:1.

I loved our family bible before I was able to read and there was a picture on the inside front cover of the Sacred Heart of Jesus; the accompanying verse, the first I learned, was Matthew 11:28. After investigating the etymology of "yoke" to be the same as yoga—uniting the human spirit with the Divine Spirit—the verse deepened dramatically for me:

> Come to me, all who labor and are heavily burdened
> And I will give you rest
> Take my yoga upon you, and learn from me
> For I am meek and humble—of the earth—in my heart, which is your heart
> And you will find rest for your soul, in which is held your mind, and your body
> Yes, my yoga is effortless and my burden is light from Light.

The chakras are implicitly referenced in numerous Christian practices; for instance, when the Gospel is introduced, Catholic say "glory to you, O Lord," and bless their forehead, their lips and their heart: the third eye, throat and heart chakras. Several writers (Tomberg, Powell, Kirchoff) have correlated the I Am statements of John's Gospel to the chakras of yoga, to powerful effect.

A lovely practice comes of this: when abiding in Awareness through dwelling as I Am, place your attention, through your intention, upon any or each of these places within you, along your central channel, several inches to the front of your spine:

I Am the resurrection and the life – John 11:25

(crown)
I Am the light of the world – John 8:12 (third eye)
I Am the good shepherd – John 10:11 (throat)
I Am the bread of life – John 6:35 (heart)
I Am the gate – John 10:9 (solar plexus)
I Am the way, the truth, and the life – John 14:6
(sacral)
I Am the true vine – John 15:1 (root)

Particularly captivating is Jesus' statement "I am the gate." Buddhism speaks of "the gateless gate"; from this side, there appears to be a gate, but once you pass through the gate and look back, there is no gate, and there never was one. Jesus too passed through the gate, looked back as Christ and beheld no gate. And he never again looked back. When Christ consciousness nears Awareness, Eckhart's "eye through which I see God is the same eye through which God sees me; my eye and God's eye are one eye, one seeing, one knowing, one love." If Jesus is the gate, then so are you, and so am I. The gateway to the heart is love, and thou art that. You and I are the gate. And Christ is the gateless gate, hara to heart.

"There is no transmigrant but the Lord," the sole Subject of all the Kosmos. "When I am not an object," says Wilber in *Always Already: the Brilliant Clarity of Ever-Present Awareness*, "I am God."

The Song of Solomon. Chap. II. v. 1-9.

AM the rose of Sharon, and the lily of the valleys.

As the lily among thorns, so is my love among the daughters.

As the apple tree among the trees of the wood, so is my beloved among the sons. I sat down under his shadow with great delight, and his fruit was sweet to my taste.

He brought me to the banqueting house, and his banner over me was love.

Stay me with flagons, comfort me with apples: for I am sick of love.

His left hand is under my head, and his right hand doth embrace me.

I charge you, O ye daughters of Jerusalem, by the roes, and by the hinds of the field, that ye stir not up, nor awake my love, till he please.

The voice of my beloved! behold, he cometh leaping upon the mountains, skipping upon the hills.

My beloved is like a roe or a young hart: behold, he standeth behind our wall, he looketh forth at the windows, shewing himself through the lattice.

The Song of Solomon.

Chap. II. v. 10-17.

My beloved spake, and said unto me, Rise up, my love, my fair one, and come away.

For, lo, the winter is past, the rain is over and gone;

The flowers appear on the earth; the time of the singing of birds is come, and the voice of the turtle is heard in our land;

The fig tree putteth forth her green figs, and the vines with the tender grape give a good smell. Arise, my love, my fair one, and come away.

O my dove, that art in the clefts of the rock, in the secret places of the stairs, let me see thy countenance, let me hear thy voice; for sweet is thy voice, and thy countenance is comely.

Take us the foxes, the little foxes, that spoil the vines: for our vines have tender grapes.

My beloved is mine, and I am his: he feedeth among the lilies.

Until the day break, and the shadows flee away, turn, my beloved, and be thou like a roe or a young hart upon the mountains of Bether.

The Lover and The Beloved

Christianity is traditionally a Spirit in 2nd-person tradition, and at times, a tepid one at that. (The words of "What a Friend we have in Jesus" come to mind, with no disrespect intended to the great old hymn.) But "Eternity is in love with the productions of time," said William Blake, and the 2nd-person traditions and practices of Christianity are stunning and sublime. The lanterns of the East, too, illuminate the room where the two of you commune, with indescribable beauty.

Our loves in the world are more than a symbol of God's love for us: *they are God's love for us, incarnate.* Our primary 2nd-person practice is to take Christ up on the injunction: "love one another as I have loved you," to incarnate God's love through the holiness of human love. Relationship is the 2nd-person practice, par excellence. And intimate human love is especially pointed to by the mystics as a way of divine love.

Nearly every translation of the Bible up until the sixteenth century was based on St. Jerome's late fourth-century translation into Latin: the *Vulgate.* One of the great contributions of modern scholarship was the ability to go back to the sources and translate freshly, anew, realizing that the original writers (and certainly the original translators) had their own context, their own hidden maps. There's some evidence, for instance, that St. Jerome translated with an agenda, to tone down what was originally written, in order to reflect the bias against the body that pervaded the axial age. That the *Song of Songs* ever made it into the Bible is a miracle to me; and in this case, the King James Version of the climax of the *Song* (straight from the Vulgate) is already erotic:

> Set me as a seal upon thine heart, as a seal upon thine arm: for love is strong as death; jealousy is cruel as the grave: the coals thereof are coals of fire, which hath a most vehement flame.

> Many waters cannot quench love, neither can the floods drown it: if a man would give all the substance of his house for love, it would utterly be contemned. (Songs 8:6-7)

Though the *Song of Songs* never refers to God (unique, amidst the books of the Bible), some delightful scholarship (Bloch and Bloch, Falk, Pope, Cantor) has looked anew at its "most vehement flame," *shal-hevetyah*, as perhaps a reference to YHWH, Israel's God. God in any case is beautifully in the background of this Book of Love, holding space for the lovers as they deepen their union and communion. The "vehement flame" of their love is understood to be *Godlike*, and the "many waters" and "floods" are understood to be the *mayim rabbim,* the great primordial waters of creation in Genesis! So in a new translation:

> Love is ferocious like death, its jealousy cruel as Sheol, its sparks, sparks of fire: a great God-flame!

> Not even the great waters of creation can extinguish the great God-flame which is love.[2]

The *Song of Songs* is an erotic text, a love story meant to model God's love for us, which is why it made its way, by stealth, into the canon. The poems of San Juan de la Cruz, St. John of the Cross—said to mark the height of Spanish language poetry—take the *Song of Songs* as their precedent. It can be experienced on your meditation cushion, in the pews of a deserted church, from the snow-capped peaks above Snowmass, or upon the holy ground to which you bring your beloved. You can know yourself to be the Beloved, or know yourself to be the Lover; these will fall away—like the garments in which you've adorned yourself—in the divine amnesia in which you simply are the Loving.

The *Song* makes God's love real, experiential, imminent, embodied, unforgettable, "a seal upon your heart." Its poetry is holy and erotic, the words themselves the foreshadow of the most breathtaking foreplay, as the dialogue of its lovers deepens, until too deep for words. The Book of Love is concealed in dusty bibles on old bookshelves, and hidden in hotel night tables, like Alladin's Lamp, waiting to be unearthed and illuminated.

In the spirit of the *Song of Songs*, we can practice partner meditation, beginning with the breath. For even breathing, David Deida tells us, is a most intimate activity. Breathing in and breathing out, we are making love with the Kosmos, though we know it not. Breathing in, Spirit pours into us, Divinity down to the dust with which we're fashioned; breathing out, Spirit leaps from that dust and returns to Divinity. Divinity and dust are deeply in love; the secret room in which they commune is the human heart, which beats in you and beats in me. If we are lovemaking in every moment, imagine the love cultivated in explicit moments of making love! The invitation is to bring your Awareness deeply and fully into your body, your breath, your energy, and to be radically present, and Presence for your beloved, who is dramatically form. There was never a more enchanting invitation to do so than with your partner, in absolute surrender and the boundless giving and receiving of love. You listen for their breath, and it comes and goes with yours; you feel their heartbeat, and it moves in time with yours. Your depth is calling to their depth, in the roar of the waterfall that cascades through you, and love's waves and breakers sweep over you.

Your hand moves from your heart to the head of your beloved. Your fingers touch her temple with the tenderness of prayer; Awareness moves embodiment to sweep aside her hair, held aside her beauty who is mirrored in your mirror: so to deepen in your gaze, as Awareness of Awareness sets embodied hearts ablaze. She whispers—in her nakedness—she's feeling overdressed; the skin is but the shimmering adorning the Caressed. Diaphanous and delicate the Body she unclothes; you Witness her, unveiling—for the lover whom she knows.

Within your Awareness, your partner is held and beheld through ever deepening states: your bodies embracing, entangling, your minds mingling, I Amness in you imbibing I Amness in your beloved, until Awareness recognizes itself and smiles. From your I Amness, collectively and effortlessly held in your mudra, one of you emerges as *Sat*: pure Being. The other of you emerges as *Chit*: pure Consciousness. Your *Sat* and their *Chit* meet in *Ananda*: pure Bliss. You two are Gibran's eternity, in the hall of *Satchitananda*, the chapel of sacred mirrors; in the gaze you share, the two of you are eternity, the two of you, the mirror.

You never break your gaze, but as you move deeper, the selves you inhabit deepen. Your body is radically present, and given to your partner's; your minds, intertwined: mingling by the mystery of the water and the wine. Abiding in consciousness—in divine amnesia—you forget who you are, and who your partner is, since you both simply *Are*. The two of you realize a miracle called We: I Am, communing with I Am, become We Are. The lover and beloved fall away, and all that remains is the Loving. And abiding in Awareness, you recognize your very self in *jnana-drishti*. You know your partner, your self, by heart, and you share an infinitely knowing, loving smile of Self-recognition, and Self-remembering.

Your feet are bared, for you've moved onto holy ground; the God-flame is not seen without, but known within, ablaze in your subtle, sacred hearts. Your beloved's heart is nearer to you than your own. Your holy embrace is an Ikon that God is writing on your sacred hearts, in the secret room, on the walls of the inner sanctum. It illuminates the Kosmos with too much love to be contained in one bed; one room; one home; one world; one Kosmos. You realize the kingdom of heaven, in your Christic heart, in your Christic mind, and you realize its perfect reflection as you touch the perfect body of your beloved, the new earth.

The Kosmic polarity that holds the universe together is pulsating between you and your partner; the energy that sent the stars flying apart moves through you into your beloved, and returns through your beloved into you. You kneel at the shoreline of the primordial waters: the chasm where one became two, and outside parted from inside, on the turning away. The two of you can bridge that gap, in your bodies, your minds, your souls, your Spirit; your secret is love, which conquers all: the God-flame which even the floods of creation cannot quench. You two become one, the outside becomes the inside in the secret room, the Holy of Holies, and there you tabernacle through your beloved, with your beloved, in your beloved. You know your partner from the inside, in *jnana-drishti*, in loving knowledge. And your partner knows you, in knowing love. The two of you are dust to Divinity, but together you realize dust-Divinity. In becoming the Other, you know the truth that there is no Other. You know the truth that you are your beloved, and your beloved is yours; and together you embody love as no one ever has, and no one ever will because the two of you are no longer two. You know the truth: "I am the Buddha we are."[4] You have Awakened together, in every sense of the word, and in that Awareness you have realized a singular vantage point and a heartbreakingly beautiful view, such that in your *metanoia*, you are never the same again. You magnify the love that your bodies were created for, that the world was created for, that the separation was created for. In your holy communion is the forgiveness of the original sin.

One of you sits as Awareness; one of you dances as *Lila*, Spirit's ecstatic play, in the midst of that Awareness. One of you holds the stillness and power of Shiva; one of you moves with the erotic embrace of

Shakti. The fragrance of your lotus pose fills the Kosmos with its sweetness. Your state deepens as you push wakefulness into the dreamy state of your art, your treasure, into the stillness state of the deep and dreamless, the slightest movement bringing waves of endless pleasure and torrents of amazing grace. Then you move together into the fourth—*turiya*—where your freedom is to eternity, and you magnify the emotion of sheer Bliss. Then you move together into the fifth—*turiyatita*—where your fullness is to infinity, and you commune in the emotion of utter Love. In your partner's waves of trembling, you feel the trembling of the entire Kosmos—you who sit as Awareness itself—and now the two of you slip into the Masterpiece. In every breath: *Hallelujah*, as you exchange self and other: in your last breath in, together you breathe in the suffering of all sentient beings, with whom you've bridged the separateness, the otherness, across the bridge you've built of love. In your last breath out, together you breathe out infinite compassion on them all, carried on the waves of Spirit's trembling, to distant shores and loving effect that you will never know, in a breath like the tonglen of Christ's, because in your passion you are breathing together as Christ, as you dance your partner to the end of Love.

Within the Wood, Beneath the Rock

Jesus knew himself to be "I Am who Am" and that "I and the Father are one." He realized the kingdom of heaven within, and with love without limit, he set about enacting the new earth without, the perfect reflection of that kingdom. He approached the three faces of God until he was on the other side of them, no longer looking *at* Spirit but looking *as* Spirit. And that Spirit is sent upon us, to illuminate the path back to Spirit.

We are invited to the same experience of God that Jesus had; according to Father Thomas, that is the purpose of the Christian tradition. We too can "be still and know that I Am God," taken quite personally. We too can enter intimately into relationship with God, knowing that we are God's beloved, and that Eternity is in love with the productions of time. The second face of God is natural to Christians; the first face, daring, but the clear injunction of Jesus' teaching, as long as by *kenosis* we are emptied of our self-sense, our exclusive identification with the self. What of the third face of God?

We saw that Jesus was a prophet of his day—he saw clearly the times, from his vantage point of states, from his view of stages. He was steeped in his culture and conversant in it. But given his realization of *states*, unpacked through his lenses of *stages*, he understood that he had no choice. If the Torah was to be fulfilled by God, it would be through Christ, whom Jesus had realized. If the Temple was to be renewed, it would be through Christ, whom Jesus embodied. If the long-expected Messiah was to come to Israel, it would be through Christ, as whom Jesus walked. Jesus understood himself to be the *enactment* of these promises; "thy kingdom come" was happening now, and "thy will be done on earth as it is in heaven" was happening here: in the knowing of heaven within, and the fashioning of the earth as its reflection without.

Jesus taught about the kingdom of heaven and the kingdom of God one hundred times in words, and his deeds (on earth as it is in heaven) were a perfect reflection of those words. In making all "on earth as it is in heaven" he was practicing Spirit in 3rd-person. If we, as per Father Thomas, are to have the same experience of God that Jesus had, we too are invited to know the kingdom of heaven within. And we too are to enact the new earth without, as its perfect reflection.

Of great interest to us is the sense of the kingdom of heaven in Thomas's Gospel. In Logion 3: "the kingdom is inside of you, and it is outside of you." This is a nondualistic view of a kingdom that is not envisioned in the end times, and not to be wrestled from the Romans in revolution; it is a kingdom that is always already present in the now, the only moment we will ever have.

In Logion 22: "Jesus said to them, 'When you make the two one, and when you make the inside like the outside and the outside like the inside, and the above like the below... then will you enter the kingdom.'"

And in Logion 77: "It is I who am the light which is above them all. It is I who am the all. From me did the all come forth, and unto me did the all extend. Split a piece of wood, and I am there. Lift up the stone, and you will find me there."

The kingdom is here and now, within you and within me. Within the wood and beneath the stone of our daily work—which is love, made visible—the kingdom has come close.

In the penultimate moment of *Ghostbusters*, our heroes are mired in the apocalypse as good makes its last stand in the face of evil. The ghostbusters discover the smoldering Sigourney Weaver, the *gatekeeper*, and then the adorably geeky Rick Moranis, the *keymaster*. Bill Murray makes the obvious connection and declares, "we've got to get these two together." Such is the nondual, found within the wood, and beneath the stone: smoldering Emptiness in yoga with adorable form.

I'll close this section on Spirit in 3rd-person with a small meditation from Ken Wilber which is so profound, we couldn't agree on which face of God it's coming through. But this is Ken Wilber, in the upper room of the Red Hill house, being one with the All:

> Raindrops are beating, a large puddle is forming, there on the balcony. It all floats in Emptiness, in pures Transparency, with no one here to watch it. If there is an I, it is all that is arising, right now and right now and right now. My lungs are the sky; those mountains are my teeth; the soft clouds are my skin; the thunder is my heart beating time to the timeless; the rain itself, the tears of our collective estate, here where nothing is really happening at all.[5]

The Secret of Thomas

The Gospel of Thomas is an *apocryphal* Gospel, which evokes a sense of an esoteric, secret teaching that very few are initiated into. Indeed, the book begins "These are the secret sayings which the living Jesus spoke and which Didymos Judas Thomas wrote down." The book was not included in the canon of the Bible, and was hidden with numerous other texts of what became the Nag Hammadi library, likely by a monk who hadn't the heart to destroy them. Thus were they protected from being burned as heretical under St. Athanasius' decree, just before St. Jerome began toning down the books that made the cut. Its author is traditionally the apostle Thomas, said to have traveled afar to India to preach the Gospel. In any case, the book is from the early school of St. Thomas.

Religious historian Elaine Pagels has pointed out that the canonical Gospel of John is almost certainly a response to the non-canonical Gospel of Thomas; for that reason alone, serious study of the Gospel is warranted, even in the most orthodox circles. We can imagine the rivalry between the early schools of John and Thomas, with John portraying Thomas as "the doubter"; Thomas, for his part, depicts his relationship with Jesus as set apart, in Logion 13:

> (1) Jesus said to his disciples: "Compare me, and tell me whom I am like."
> (2) Simon Peter said to him: "You are like a just messenger."
> (3) Matthew said to him: "You are like an (especially) wise philosopher."
> (4) Thomas said to him: "Teacher, my mouth cannot bear at all to say whom you are like."
> (5) Jesus said "I am not your teacher. For you have drunk, you have become intoxicated at the bubbling spring that I have measured out."
> (6) And he took him, (and) withdrew, (and) he said three words to him.
> (7) But when Thomas came back to his companions, they asked him: "What did Jesus say to you?"
> (8) Thomas said to them: "If I tell you one of the words he said to me, you will pick up stones and throw them at me, and fire will come out of the stones (and) burn you up."

The secret of Thomas was never revealed to his companions; the secret of Thomas was never revealed in his Gospel. We are left to wonder what the three words were, that Jesus said to Thomas. I believe I know what they were.

Jesus' name (perhaps better translated "Joshua") is a combination of two Hebrew words; the beginning shares the same letters as the name of Israel's God YH-WH—I Am who Am. The ending of his name means "saves," or literally "rescues." So his name means "I Am who Am, and it is I that rescues."

These words are mysterious and ambiguous. "Jesus saves" is something you might see on a placard in the end zone of a football stadium to catch the camera in an attempt to evangelize, even while a field goal is being attempted. But in my mind it goes much deeper. The name "I Am who Am" rescues, precisely because "I Am" is the bridge between consciousness and Awareness, or between Christ Consciousness and God Consciousness. As we abide in consciousness, we realize that we have a mind, and we have a body (the reflection of our mind). Once we realize we have these, we are free of them, and more—they can be poured out in *kenosis* and given to God, in the service of love. But in questioning "who am I?" of that self, the True Self, we can say very little: simply "I Am," but said with absolute certainty. The true Self of Jesus is Christ, but that implies that your true Self, my true Self too is Christ: "Verily, there is no other transmigrant but the Lord." "I Am who Am" is a name but it is also an injunction: "Be still, and know that I Am." That is the path that Jesus took; he knew the truth "I Am." And that is the path that Ramana Maharshi took; he too knew the truth "I Am." The Secret of Thomas is "YHWH rescues," and Jesus' message is "take my yoga upon you"—know your own I Amness—and you will find rest for your soul, which holds your mind, which holds your body; your soul, which abides in Awareness. "YHWH," *I Am*, is the secret of Thomas.

That is the secret of Thomas the Twin; but then there is Thomas the Trappist, and he bore a secret too. Thomas Keating was a giant in his vast mind and contemplative heart, who came into God's presence on the rising tide of silence. In his white Trappist robes and his towering stature, he reminded me of Tolkien's Gandalf the White. He surely put on the mind of Christ, and loved with the most Sacred Heart. He lived to ninety-five years of age, and ran what he adorably called a "three-ring circus" of monastic life, inter-religious dialogue and contemplative outreach. Though he was the abbot of a Cistercian Trappist monastery (the order of Sister Maria from *The Sound of Music*, among the strictest orders of the Catholic

Church), he audaciously invited Japanese Rinzai Zen Master Sasaki Jōshū to give meditation retreats to his monks in the 1970's. He distilled the contemplative practice of Catholicism (*Lectio Divina*) into the sublimely simple practice of Centering Prayer, which he shared with quite literally millions of people over the last decades of his life. He said of the prayer: "Centering prayer is all about heartfulness, which is a little different from mindfulness."

In Centering Prayer, we choose a *sacred word* which symbolizes our deep and complete intention to surrender to God, to approach God *on God's terms, whatever that means*, and to be present, in and as Rahner's "infinite emptiness" to the "infinite fullness" that is God. As we move into the presence of God, we introduce the sacred word, and then simply stay present: "be still and know that I Am God." The sacred word is not repeated as a mantra; it's gently reintroduced as our monkey minds do what they do, and we return to silence, and to presence. We do this as often as needed through our time of practice; Father Thomas suggested a time frame of at least twenty minutes to come into the depth that the Divine invites us to. He loved Matthew 6:6, as an injunction to contemplation:

But whenever you pray, go into your room and shut the door and pray to your Father who is in secret; and your Father who sees in secret will reward you.

We approach God with the trust that we are on holy ground, and that our intention to approach God on God's terms is always received: a prayer that is always answered. To the impossible injunction of "be perfect as your Father in heaven is perfect," Thomas Merton (Thomas Keating's friend, contemporary and Cistercian brother) adds:

> ...this then is what it means to seek God perfectly: to withdraw from illusion and pleasure, from worldly anxieties and desires, from the works that God does not want, from a glory that is only human display; to keep my mind free from confusion in order that my liberty may be always at the disposal of his will; to entertain silence in my heart and listen for the voice of God; to cultivate an intellectual freedom from the images of created things in order to receive the secret contact of God in obscure love; to love all people as myself; to rest in humility and to find peace in withdrawal from conflict and competition with other men; to turn aside from controversy and put away

heavy loads of judgement and censorship and criticism and the whole burden of opinions that I have no obligation to carry; to have a will that is always ready to fold back within itself and draw all the powers of the soul down from its deepest center to rest in silent expectancy for the coming of God, poised in tranquil and effortless concentration upon the point of my dependence of him; to gather all that I am, and have all that I can possibly suffer or do or be, and abandon them all to God in the resignation of a perfect love and blind faith and pure trust in God, to do his will. And then to wait in peace and emptiness and oblivion of all things.

Bonum est praestolari cum silentio salutare Dei.

It is good to wait in silence for the salvation of God.[6]

Father Thomas emerged from a lifetime of contemplative prayer and the dusty books penned by the Christian contemplatives of the ages, and wove them into a simple teaching that moved millions. He adapted the practice to include other sacred symbols that might work powerfully for people, depending on their type and temperament: the sacred breath and the sacred image.

At an Integral Spiritual Center event, Thomas Keating—a giant among contemplatives—and Ken Wilber—a giant among philosophers—met for an unforgettable sharing. The event began with Wilber telling the crowd who'd gathered of Father Thomas's singular contribution to dusting off contemplative practice—which had waned since the Council of Trent (with the Catholic Church entrenching in formulaic dogmas to defend itself from the perceived offence of the Reformation)—and sharing it with the world. Wilber "spoke in paragraphs" about the impact of Father Thomas's 70 years as a contemplative in action, to the crowd's deeply moved delight. When he'd finished, the room fell silent, and Father Thomas smiled and said "so what shall we talk about today?" Wilber came back with a stupendous reply, deadpanning, "I noticed you resisted the temptation to say something nice about me..."

And in fact, at the inaugural Integral Spiritual Center gathering, Father Thomas offered Wilber one of the deepest tributes I've ever heard. He referred to the fact that kensho, satori, moksha, liberation, enlightenment are sometimes assumed to be impossible to talk about, due to their profundity, "too deep for words." But Ken Wilber, said Father Thomas, "gave us the words, the vocabulary with which to share the Mystery." Father Thomas acknowledged Wilber as having contributed immensely from afar to the groundbreaking Snowmass Interspiritual Dialogues, simply due to the clarity, audaciousness and grandeur of his thought.

As Father Thomas deepened his own practice, he came upon a sacred symbol that was deeper still than the sacred word, the sacred image, the sacred breath: the *sacred nothing*.

Father Thomas taught that the whole purpose of the Christian tradition was to come into the same relationship with God that Jesus had, the transcendent as imminent, and intimate ("Abba"). In the moving Snowmass Interspiritual Dialogues, he ever sought a term that all present could agree upon, in referring to the Divine; he himself loved "the Mystery." He frequently emphasized that God is *no thing*, and in lighter moments, proposed that we give the indescribable *I Am who Am* an affectionate nickname: *Izzy!* Awareness—which Father Thomas enthroned and embodied—took the *sacred nothing* as object, in an incomparably profound activity: Gibran's eternity gazing at itself in the mirror, with you, eternity, and you, the mirror.

A famous Zen Koan originates with the legendary meeting between Master Bodhidharma and Emperor Liang Wu. When the Emperor asked, "What is the ultimate meaning of the sacred teaching?" the Master is said to have replied, "Vast emptiness; nothing sacred!" The secret of Thomas is the answer to the Koan of *nothing sacred*: the *sacred nothing*.

Icon of Holy Women: St. Paraskevi, St. Varvara, St. Akaterini, St. Thekla, St. Marina

"Christ the True Vine"
(16th century Greek icon)

"Ladder of Divine Ascent," Monastery of St. Catherine, Sinai
(12th century)

Figure 1: Stages of Faith

summarized from James Fowler, *Stages of Faith* (1995)

0. *Primal Faith*	Primal faith or undifferentiated faith unfolds in infancy, from birth to two years of age. This stage begins prior to the emergence of language and conceptual thought, as the infant forms a basic sense of trust and of being at home in the world. The infant forms "pre-images" of God, or the Holy, and what kind of world they live in. Crucially, this basic trust or mistrust forms the foundation for the later unfolding of faith. Says Fowler, "Future religious experience will either have to confirm or reground that basic trust."
1. *Intuitive-Projective Faith*	Intuitive-projective faith characterizes the child of two to six or seven. Faith in this stage is changing, growing and dynamic. It's a time of imagination; the child doesn't yet employ the sort of logic that would make questioning of their fantasies necessary, or even possible. The child's mind at this stage, says Fowler, is "religiously pregnant." The experiences and images that take form prior to six have powerful, enduring effects on the life of faith, in positive and negative ways.

2. Mythic-Literal Faith	Mythic-literal faith brings about a new way of dealing with the world; making meaning now involves evaluating and criticizing the imagination and fantasy of the intuitive-projective stage. This is a stage of narrative, with the individual at this stage able to weave together powerful stories that capture their meaning making. The stories are literal, though, and the individual is not yet able to step outside the stories and reflect upon their meanings. Symbols and myths are taken at face value, though they may be moving at a deeper level.
3. Synthetic-Conventional Faith	Synthetic-conventional faith typically emerges beginning around 12 or 13. This stage coincides with Piaget's formal operational thinking (one is able to think about thinking). Forming an identity is the hallmark of this stage; one is concerned about what significant others are thinking about them. The "synthetic" refers to the pulling together one's valued images and values into a sense of self or identity. Images of God tend to be extensions of personal interpersonal relationships: God as "Friend, Companion and Personal Reality," in whom I'm deeply known and valued. This valuing serves as guarantor of one's identity and worth in a world in which one is struggling to discover who they are.

4. Individu-ative-Reflective Faith	At the individuative-reflective stage, the individual steps away from the interpersonal circles which have formed them to that point, and begins to reflect on themselves as separate from those circles and the world they shared, and which defined them. If one was a "fish in water" in the third stage, the individual at this stage has sprung outside the tank and is reflecting on the water from which they sprang. Many people never complete the transition, and remain caught in between these stages. At this stage—usually commencing in young adulthood—boundaries are paramount, and the individual is concerned about authenticity and fit between the selves they feel themselves to be and the ideological commitments of the groups they involve themselves in.
5. Conjunctive Faith	In midlife some people undergo a change to a conjunctive faith, which is more permeable and porous than the boundaried identity of the previous stage. One is aware that the conscious self is not all there is, and that one's behavior is shaped by dimensions that one is not fully aware of. One at this stage deepens in their readiness for a relationship with God, which includes both God's mystery, unavailability and strangeness and God's closeness and clarity.

5. **Conjunctive** **Faith** [cont'd]	The looking into one's own unconsciousness is accompanied by a looking into the social unconsciousness—the myths, taboos and standards we took in with our mother's milk—and how powerfully that shapes oneself and others. With this reflection one is ready for new intimacy with people and groups different from oneself, and, says Fowler, "allegiances beyond our tribal gods and tribal taboos." At this stage, it is understood that truth has many dimensions, to be held together in paradoxical tension.
6. **Universal-** **izing** **Faith**	Some few persons move into Universalizing Faith. People at this stage begin to radically live as though what Christians and Jews call "the kingdom of God" were already a fact. It's quite beyond these images though—there is a shift from self as the center of experience, as the center becomes a participation in God or Ultimate Reality. "There's a reversal of figure and ground," says Fowler, and these individuals are at home in a commonwealth of being. They are at the same time more lucid and simple than we are, and intensely liberating, even subversive. They negate the self for the sake of affirming God, and in doing so became powerful and vibrant selves in our experience.

SIX

THE MIND OF CHRIST

*I*sometimes sadly smile that the parts of the Bible that were always intended as a story are taken literally, and the parts that were written as though your life depended on them—because it does—are overlooked and passed by. A progressive political campaign in Canada, running against a fundamentalist Christian candidate, declared the devastating, rational truth: "*The Flintstones* was not a documentary"; nor, by extension, is the Book of Genesis. The Bible—as Ken Wilber brilliantly observed, the "blog of God"— was written over several thousand years, by many different authors who allowed Awareness to inhabit their consciousness and to move their minds and bodies to record what they'd received from where they were at. We read the musings of an angry, impetuous teenager in some of the earlier scriptures, and words of astounding, mature spiritual wisdom in the later books. Humanity was growing up as it wrote the Bible, and modern scholarship again provides profound lenses with which to make meaning of the words long written down.

The book of Genesis is liberated when we allow it to be what it was always meant to be: a beautiful allegory rather than a literal (and self-contradictory) history of the world. By contrast, Jesus repeatedly spoke of the kingdom: the "kingdom of God" occurs 68 times and the "kingdom of heaven" 32 times. Bible scholars generally agree that whereas certain words might have been put in the mouth of Jesus by the authors of the Gospels, he almost certainly preached about the kingdom, and he meant what he said. The injunction *metanoia*—change your mind—was mentioned by John the Baptist as he prepared the way of the Lord, by Jesus himself as he began his ministry, and by St. Paul: you must "put on the mind of Christ, who, though he was in the form of God, did not deem equality with some something to cling to; rather he emptied himself..." The necessary injunction of Christianity is to change your mind, to go beyond it, to GROW UP. This is meant deeply and completely literally. And the deeper mind to come into is the mind of Christ.

Monkey Mind, Metamind, Mirror Mind

I recall being at a meditation teaching with the instruction to count to 10, then return to 1 and count again to 10, repeatedly for 30 minutes. When the closing bell rang, I turned to my friend who said "I couldn't even make it to 8!" to which I responded "I had no problem at all getting to 14!" We are so thoroughly in our minds that we don't ordinarily realize we have a mind; our minds have us, and that is monkey mind.

Though monkey-mind refers to what is effectively our default *state* of consciousness, it also tends to be our starting point when we re-embark on the journey through *stages* of consciousness. If we haven't consciously continued the developmental journey we began in school, we likely haven't really taken in that we *have* a mind, nor the implications of that: what do we do with that mind, and *who are we*, in the first place? To the question of what to do with that mind, we can cultivate and develop it, and take into our hands the hidden map that we've always, if unconsciously, been following. The journey is long and arduous, and becomes increasingly the road less travelled. The hidden map is invaluable for finding our way to the most expansive view we can possibly take, and from there to embody love with freedom, and with fullness.

Our society tends to move us up through developmental stages (via education and socialization) and once we reach the center of gravity of the culture we're embedded in, our growth can slow or come to a standstill, since society is no longer encouraging and facilitating that growth. We are, as Robert Kegan said, essentially in "developmental arrest." And worse, should we attempt to venture into later stages, our culture will tend to draw us back to the center of gravity.

What this means, in this place and time, is to embark upon the long journey through developmental *stages*, in the footsteps of Jesus who undertook that journey in his case. But in our case, the journey looks very different; whereas in Jesus' time, the mythic stage had emerged and beyond that: a trackless land in which Christ blazed a trail of love. In our case, the rational stage has emerged, the pluralistic stage, and the Integral stages of teal and turquoise. And even the formerly trackless land of the 3rd-tier stages has begun to take form as para-mind, meta-mind, overmind and Supermind. The perfect person, says Chuang

Tzu, employs the mind as a mirror. It neither grasps nor rejects; it receives, but does not keep." The most panoramic vantage point is from the realized nondual state; the most expansive view is from the mirror mind of the Supermind stage.

"Putting on the mind of Christ" in our case means to follow in the footsteps of Jesus and beyond. "Working out our salvation" includes taking wider and wider apertures in an "I" that is increasingly spacious, and a "we" that is increasingly inclusive, until every human being, and every being is included, without exception. And an "it" that means "the kingdom of heaven" *within* reflects and enacts the new earth *without*. When it comes to being, "all sentient beings" form the community of the adequate.

There is another reason to take up Jesus' injunction of "I Am the way." Even as we move from our gross heart, to our subtle, sacred heart—in which all the beauty and tragedy of our lives blossom and come to bloom—to our most Sacred Heart, which we share with all human beings—since the number of transmigrants is one—we take an increasingly stunning vista. The jump of Spirit takes a vantage point of the Kosmos, ever more wondrously as we consciously experience the return. But even as we find increasingly profound vantage points on the valley, we take ever more sublime views. The view will unpack the vantage point in increasingly faithful ways; to the extent that we have followed Jesus' example of moving through *stages* of consciousness, we will lose less of our *state* of consciousness in translation. If we want to get Christ's message—and this applies to every person on the spiritual journey—we need to have ears to hear it and eyes to see it. The kingdom of heaven is only fully received by the new earth, and the most Sacred Heart is definitively, completely, and endlessly known-loved in the mind of Christ.

Whereas our journey through states is as old as humanity, and tread by every human every day and every night, our journey through stages—though it too has evolved from the start—was only recently spotted, with the lenses of modernity. We best honour the vantage point of our *state* by taking the most profound view of the *stage* we've come into; or conversely, the deepest move we can make from the *stage* we've reached is to immerse it, and ourselves, in the deepest *state* we can practice. These states and stages unfold in increasingly profound ways: omniscience is the signature quality of the latest *stage* that we are aware of, and the Risen Christ, by whatever name, is the summit of the *states* of consciousness.

The Ladder of Jacob

We saw, as we walked with Jesus, that stages of human development—themselves afforded to us by the postmodern stage of consciousness—are seen clearly by asking questions: who am I? of what am I aware? what is of ultimate concern? and watching the answers, over time. When we look closely, we find patterns in the answers to each of these questions. As large groups of people are seen from this *view from the outside* over periods of time, developmentalists are able to discern where people are at, and what can be expected in their further unfolding. To "who am I?" the answers show an increasingly expansive identity, until the answer is "I Am" (omnipotence). To the question of "of what am I aware?" the answers become more complete, until "everything, from my particular aperture" (omniscience). And to the question "what is of ultimate concern?" the answer asymptotically approaches the inescapable conclusion: God.

While the notion of development has been

around for millennia, its modern iteration is scarcely a century old. Structuralism gave researchers, for the first time, an outside view of the interior of the individual (as opposed to the ancient practice of introspection, which gives the inside view of the interior of the individual). The numerous lines of development originate from the types of questions that various researchers posed.

Particularly interesting were the questions that James Fowler—recipient of the inaugural Integral Spiritual Center award—posed, regarding faith, or how people make meaning. Fowler asked his respondents questions such as "what do the scriptures mean," or, in a fascinating twist, "where do the scriptures come from?" Using Jean Gebser's cognitive stages of development (archaic / magic / mythic / mental / integral), the answers unfold predictably. People at the mythic stage of development often respond that "God wrote the Bible"; at the rational level, it becomes all too clear that human beings were the authors. At pluralistic, the answer might be that humans wrote the scriptures, but under divine inspiration. And what might we say from the Integral level?

The Integral level is the first to spot the fact that

as we develop, we continually make subject into object, abiding in increasingly expansive and spacious subjects. Speculation—and the testimony of a precious few witnesses—points to a point at which all subjects have been made object, and we finally come to rest as Absolute Subjectivity: in other words, as Spirit Itself. When we look from a place of infinite depth, through a kaleidoscope of infinite perspectives, it is Spirit that is writing these words, and Spirit that is reading them....

From this view, it is indeed God who wrote the scriptures—but God by means of human perspectives, human contexts, human limitations. As human beings evolved, so did their perspectives—or the perspectives that God was able to take through their eyes. Scripture itself is evidence of this; the older books of the Bible bear the hallmarks of magical consciousness; later books begin to evidence mythical consciousness and beyond. In so many ways, scripture is simply a record of Spirit's own unfolding: Wilber's "God as blogger."

Wilber suggests that this line of development—the spiritual line, is unique among the lines of development in its endpoint. The spiritual line of development runs from dust to Divinity: its realm is infinity, its timeline eternity. James Fowler's *Stages of Faith* are described in Figure 1. Note that adults can be found at any of Fowler's Stages 2 through 6:

> At any of the stages from two on you can find adults who are best described by these stages. We do find many persons, in churches and out, who are best described by faith that essentially took form when they were adolescents.[1]

Having the "hidden map" of James Fowler's stages of faith is an immense blessing of being in our times. The first light of dawn is falling on the mountain trail upon which we walk, and we can begin to see and navigate the path in a new way, as never before. We can look to the stages we know are to follow, and recognize them inside ourselves, and not be afraid to move toward them, and resource ourselves for them. We can begin to know where others are at, too, on the journey with the hidden map, and to have compassion on them, and scaffold and assist them when the time is right. Sometimes the words *not* said in the homily, or the confessional, are the most powerful—and you will begin to recognize those. And you will know the profundity of "who am I to judge?"

In the microgeny of the moment, every *now* arrives in nondual perfection. It can be prehended in that perfection, from the Supermind stage (Wilber's highest stage): the most expansive view, taken in from the most profound vantage point. But few of us have ever inhabited that vantage point or taken that view; we are earlier on our journeys. So we miss the moment from there and it cascades down, like falling down a staircase. We finally catch the moment from precisely the stage we have stabilized and the state we're in. It's still perfect, but seems less so—something is lost in translation and we know the pain of feeling several states removed, several stages apart from the nondual perfection of the *now*, which always already *is*. Our twin journeys through states and stages can help us meet the moment as Christ does.

In retrospect, Jesus walked this path until the path ended, at which point he blazed a new trail, which arrives at the "gateless gate." The man took the deepest possible view from the highest possible vantage point, and shattered the Kosmic habit that "when we die, we remain dead" so dramatically that we're still talking about him and wondering what the hell happened. But it's all in his very name: *I Am rescues*. Turn your consciousness (which is Christ Consciousness) toward

Awareness itself; empty your vast Christic mind, and most Sacred Heart. There, the eye through which you see God is the same eye through which God sees you: one eye, one sight, and one knowledge, one love. There, heaven and earth are inescapably intertwined and entangled; there, divinity meets humanity; there, the kingdom is come, and it is on earth as it is in heaven.

To follow in the footsteps of Jesus—which is all he ever asked us to do—to walk a mile in his sandals, or just as well, our John Fleuvogs, we need to take the highest possible perspective we can, in every case, and then to act definitively: turn the tables before us, and draw the line in the sand in our midst. We need to walk in our world as we were, but never turn a blind eye; do the same as we did, but never miss a moment, or our chance to add to that moment the novel emergent of nothing but love. It could be to learn a new language. It could be to learn about the catastrophic history of the indigenous people of your place, and to stand with them in solidarity. "God bless Elijah, with a feather in his hand…" was sung of Elijah Harper, an indigenous Canadian politician who singlehandedly blocked a new national constitutional accord by standing with an eagle feather and softly saying "no", because the accord neglected to acknowledge the rights of the nations that lived in Canada, before there was Canada. It could be to acknowledge the systemic racism that Lincoln addressed, that MLK was killed for, and that has shifted forms until this day, because it refused to pass away, as all things must.

Moving through stages of development is simply opening your aperture (which is Awareness Itself looking through your consciousness—the same as Christ's—to enliven your mind and animate your body) until your perspective approaches God's perspective, because you have surrendered your mind and moved into *metanoia*, beyond the mind, metamind. But now your consciousness *has* a mind, which is liberated to take every perspective of every being into whose midst your way unfolds. To transcend-and-include them all. Your Christ consciousness has a mind with which to discern, to draw the line in the sand that you know you must draw, when you summon its wisdom: your sublime mind of Christ. And it has a heart, a body, with which to turn the tables you know you must turn, when you summon its courage: your ferocious, most Sacred Heart.

Holy Ground

The states we inhabit and stabilize (seen from within) and the stages that we journey through (seen from without) bring us to the vantage point we experience the Kosmos from, and deliver the view we can take from there. Those following the way of embodied love are quite literally invited by the Divine to contemplate the Kosmos with the mind of Christ, and to love her every being with the most Sacred Heart. That is what Jesus did, and taught others to do: "You will do the things I have done, and you will do greater things than these, since I am going to the Father."

That statement of Jesus always captivated me. How could we possibly do "greater things than these," considering the line in the sand and the turning of the tables, the blind who could see and the captives, free? When I understood what it meant to put on the mind of Christ, and did so in my case, I began to see: the mind of Christ has centuries more experience of experience than it did when Jesus inhabited it. The mind of Christ has evolved, through rational, through pluralistic, through Integral. The mind of Christ has developed into transrational awareness, as Jesus, the other sages of the ages, and the holy women and men after them ventured there and laid down tracks; that tier is slowly taking shape. Jesus' invitation was to put on the mind of Christ, to fearlessly take that perspective, to move with wisdom and compassion in the world, with the knowledge that we gain from that perspective. And even to work with *and as* Christ in our case, to further make the way of embodied love, to infuse it with the spectacularly unique fragrance of our lives and our love, and to set lanterns out for those coming after us.

In his *Categorical Imperative*, the prolific Idealist thinker Immanuel Kant echoed the Golden Rule—which exists in some form in most of the world's great traditions—as though in a hall of mirrors:

> Act only according to that maxim whereby you can, at the same time, will that it should become a universal law.[2]

Kant's imperative makes perfect sense in the light of Integral thinking. In our analogy of Spirit's dive, if you're reading these words, you're likely near the top of the painting in your return to Spirit, where the canvas turns transparent, and you begin to see details of the valley never spotted before, and to paint what you see, rather than taking the painting as given. This is holy ground, where few have walked before you and many will follow in your footsteps.

The Buddha from the Future

At the end of a supremely sublime retreat, the room fell silent, and Ken Wilber, who'd held space during those days, gave a closing thought, with no hesitation: "treat every being as though they were a Buddha from the future." I knew in that moment that he had given a new Categorical Imperative, that Wilber had moved as Kant, in his case, and that, though we'd not begun to live Kant's words, Wilber had given us new words to live by.

My understanding of Jesus' life is that he followed in his tradition to its beautiful endpoint; that he followed the hidden map of stages so that he understood well his times—a prophet is not one who sees the future, but rather one who sees the present, with clarity—and he dove so deeply into the realization of states that he landed on the other side of the eye through which he saw God, such that God saw him; that he passed through the gate and looked back to where there never was a gate: the gateless gate. The man with a lion's heart looked up and met the lion's gaze of God who looked down. Jesus recognized that the love of God would have its greatest effect in the realm of humanity, tabernacled in his Sacred Heart, and that if "thy kingdom come" and "thy will be done, on earth as it is in heaven"—the words he gave his disciples when they asked him to teach them to pray— were to mean anything, were to be true, were to be fulfilled, they would have to be so through him. Christ was Formless, but Jesus took the matter into his own hands.

We Shall See Him as He Is

> See what love the Father has given us, that we should be called children of God; and that is what we are. The reason the world does not know us is that it did not know him. Beloved, we are God's children now; what we will be has not yet been revealed. What we do know is this: when he is revealed, we will be like him, for we will see him as he is. (1 John 3:1-2)

We often hear that we are "children of God," but John, who has accompanied us on our journey through states and stages, tells us that is just the beginning. At any of the 3rd-tier structures, *what we do know is that we will be like him, for we will see him as he is*. The implications of this are lifechanging. *We shall see him as he is*: the body and mind of Jesus, abiding in Christ Consciousness which is abiding in Awareness. And *we shall be like him*: our own precious human birth, in this body and this mind (our souls finding rest), abiding in Christ Consciousness, abiding in Awareness. Seeing him as he is implies that we will be at the same Kosmic Address (KA) as Christ, and as Wilber says of this case:

> Because the subject and object in this highest case are in full resonance (possess the same KA), they will be able to be realized in a state of samadhi, or mystical unity, which means their KAs overlap directly and immediately.[3]

Awareness is ever seeking Awareness in self-recognition. Awareness came through love into consciousness, which had the idea of the mind, and the heart. And every heart will return to love, Leonard Cohen reminds us, though they return as refugees.

To be more specific, God Consciousness creates, in Its simple knowing-as-loving, or loving-as-knowing. Its perfect reflection (as Its creations are in Its image and likeness) is Christ Consciousness in all sentient beings, projected into the Kosmos through

Spirit's involution. The Word is made flesh. At the bottom of the jump, Spirit awakens as a sentient being with a mind and a body, in amnesia from the jump, of its identity as Spirit. But there are footprints in the sand, and footprints in the snow: a clue of the Alpha, where the journey began in love; and pointing to the Omega, where the journey will end in love. Christ Consciousness is drawn to God Consciousness with magnetic attraction, like the gravity between heavenly bodies. Jesus and his holy sisters and brothers made that journey, through the gateless gate of Christ and to its endpoint, where the flesh is made Word; they themselves are the way. And Christ sent the Spirit so that we might see the footprints, find the trail, and light lanterns along the way. The Spirit that moves us is the Spirit of evolution.

To treat every being as a Buddha from the future is to recognize, with your Christ consciousness, the Christ in every being, to know that Christ is present in the least of Christ's sisters and brothers.

At that time the disciples came to Jesus and asked, "Who is the greatest in the kingdom of heaven?" He called a child, whom he put among them, and said, "Truly I tell you, unless you change and become like children, you will never enter the kingdom of heaven. Whoever becomes humble like this child is the greatest in the kingdom of heaven. Whoever welcomes one such child in my name welcomes me. (Matthew 18: 3-5)

The least of Christ's sisters and brothers is the greatest in the kingdom of heaven, and the meek and humble—like Jesus, whose heart is of the earth, whose yoga is easy—will inherit the earth. But the kingdom is *here*, the only place we will ever be, and the kingdom is *now*, the only moment we will ever have. The kingdom of heaven is the perfect realization of Christ, in emptiness; the new earth is the perfect reflection of that realization, in form. And thou art that.

SEVEN

A CITY ON A HILL

The Parable of the Hundred Pesos

We all start with 100 pesos. We have 100 pesos to invest in our development along the twin trajectories of states and stages. When, as we saw earlier, part of our self cannot make the jump, it splits off and remains at the stage it's at. If 10 pesos split off at one of the first three big jumps, by definition you form a psychosis, borderline disorder or neurosis. And the self, in charge of keeping our selves together, needs to spend an equal amount of energy repressing the split off self, just to function in the world. You now have only 80 pesos with which to make the journey through states and stages; shadow is devastatingly costly. In the birth canal, we nearly die, and life doesn't get any easier from there.

We're freely offered the most Sacred Heart with which to experience God as Jesus did: the transcendent as imminent, the uttermost as intimate. We're freely offered the mind of Christ: to know ourselves within as the kingdom of heaven and ourselves without as the new earth, not to *see* God but rather to *be* God. (Wilber: When I am not an object, I am God.) We were born to bear these, as prophesied by Ezekiel: "I will give you a new heart and put a new spirit in you." We were born to bear the heart and mind of Christ, in our very body, as prophesied by Meister Eckhart: "We are all meant to be mothers of God." The most Sacred Heart and the mind of Christ are our birthright: the true heart and the true mind of the true Self, which is Christ. It is to us—all of us—that they have been bequeathed. It's only with "body, mind, soul and Spirit" that we can "love the Lord your God with all your heart, and all your mind, and all your soul, and all your strength." We enact his injunction by embarking on the long journey through states (WAKE UP, in heart), stages (GROW UP, in mind), shadow (CLEAN UP, in soul), and strength (SHOW UP, in all four quadrants, becoming Christ in our case).

But shadow can—and almost by default, will—

waylay us on the way to where Christ longs to say, "Come, you who are blessed by my Father, inherit the kingdom prepared for you from the foundation of the world. For I was hungry…" when the Man comes around. The longer we live, the more of our pesos are locked up, invested in split off selves and the "Master" trying to keep it together, repressing the split off selves like an overwhelmed juggler because we can't function in the world as them. We can no longer see clearly:

> Or how can you say to your neighbor, 'Let me take the speck out of your eye,' while the log is in your own eye? (Matthew 7:4)

In our present mental health crisis, shadow is collectively overtaking light. And yet, the darkness is yielding; part of the good news in this day and age— apart from "bring Awareness into waking, dreaming and deep sleep" and "inhabit the highest view you can possibly take, and then act decisively from there" —is the truth "it's OK to not be OK."

Sometimes it's said that our most precious commodity is time, and that we have the same number of hours in a day than did Newton, Einstein, Mother Teresa. But there may be a deeper truth here: Jesus, whom we've considered in *Christ in History*, ministered for a scant three years and was believed to have died at the young age of 33. Perhaps rather than time, *energy* is our most precious commodity. Human creativity, ingenuity and love are inexplicably boundless, given our apparent boundaries. But when we know that Awareness animates our Consciousness, which gives life to our minds and raises our bodies, we know that we are inexhaustible at the source.

When we've forgotten who we truly Are, we can become lost in our mind and trapped in our body, which were never meant to take on a separate self-sense, and are in fact our two great vehicles for embodying love in the world, which is precisely the realm of love. Our energy is precious, and our consciousness has access to the incalculable and inexhaustible energy of the Kosmos, if we can abide in the Awareness from which we are sourced. When every door has closed, there is ever a window, which liberates your life energy and gives you manna for the journey, through the wilderness of stages, through the desert of states: CLEAN UP.

The Darkness, Not Understood

Ken Wilber's precision and clarity are helpful here. In normal development, per Robert Kegan, the *subject* of one stage becomes the *object* of the subject of the next stage. When some part of the self cannot make the jump, part of the subject literally refuses to become an object. No one is to blame—perhaps that part of the subject was too shattered to become an object. So usually the "I" of one stage becomes a "me" or a "mine" to the next stage; when development goes wrong, a subpersonality either remains embedded in the central "I" (fixation) or splits off as a sub-I (dissociation). Both of these are unconscious, and neither are a proper object of awareness of the new subject. The breakage (subpersonality) and its effects (repression) are unconscious, but costly; and worse, the costs are unseen to the self. Development is always "transcend and include," and here, in all of us, either the transcend or the include are broken. And thus, we, our selves, are broken.

Various versions of the sublime prologue to John's Gospel translate "the light shines in the darkness, and the darkness has not overcome it" as "the light shines in the darkness, and the darkness has not *understood*

it." This is enlightening to our consideration of shadow. At any given fulcrum of stages or switchpoint of
states, the self (or a substantial part of the self) is ready
to transcend and include, coming into a later stage or
deeper state. That part of the self *prehends* the previous part and *comprehends* its new way of being, its
later self, its deeper self. The part that can't make the
jump fails to comprehend the new self, and splits off
from it. It too is quite literally in over its head.

That said, we too, as light in ourselves, have failed
to understand the darkness in ourselves. Our shadow
is by definition our blind spot, and by default we're
not aware of its presence in us, that it consumes our
life force simply by maintaining itself, that it requires
still more life force to repress it so as to maintain some
semblance of functioning in the world. Part of the
work is to go back to the beginning; to understand
where the heartbreak began. This can be on our own,
with a beloved, with a trusted friend, or with a ther-
apist.

In the beautiful image of our stages of meaning
being represented as *matryoshkas*—nested Russian
dolls—as opposed to a rigid ladder, part of ourselves
broke off as we neared the time to make our momen-

tous leap; perhaps she froze at the fear of the jump. There is a tiny matryoshka within, frightened and alone, precisely where we left her on our momentous leap. She is no less Spirit than the self that made the jump; she is the least of our sisters and brothers, and therefore the least of Christ's. "Let the little ones come to me," he said. She is deserving of our knowing, and our loving; she has a message for us, in service of our growth. And she longs to return to the light of our life: the lost sheep, of whom Jesus spoke: "which of you would not leave the ninety-nine behind, to go after the lost one?"

The Way is Shut

At some point, every one of us encounters the inscription at the haunted pass by which our heroes, Aragorn, Legolas and Gimli, make the journey from Rohan to Gondor, in Tolkien's *The Lord of the Rings: The Return of the King*:

> The way is shut. It was made by those who are Dead, and the Dead keep it, until the time comes. The way is shut.[1]

Your development has come to an end, as your life force—in theory, infinite—is spent in shadows, and keeping them hidden. We are, all of us, legion. And the most Sacred Heart and Christlike mind that were the first thoughts of God, when God spoke the Word, are now barely out of your reach. No matter how much you long to know Christ in your mind and love Christ in your heart, you have nowhere to go. *You yourself are God's shadow.* Your next step is necessarily to face your shadow, to "liberate the captives" of Isaiah that Christ fulfilled in the reading and the sermon at Nazareth.

The injunction, from the Divine, comes in the words of Jesus, from his mind of Christ:

> You are the light of the world. A city built on a hill cannot be hid. No one after lighting a lamp puts it under the bushel basket, but on the lampstand, and it gives light to all in the house. In the same way, let your light shine before others... (Matthew 5:15-16)

I suffered a trauma at around the age of five. For decades I rationalized it—from my rational, explaining it away as "nothing"—though I viscerally shuddered every time I walked by the place where it took place, and my most loved ones tried with all their hearts to help me understand its effects. My way was shut, and my blind spot was that it was so. I was in developmental arrest and worse: I lost whom I loved most to world with. And was inconsolably heartbroken at not being able to bring a giftedness I knew within myself to the world.

At long last I dove deeply into discovering the darkness, and contacting the utter shatteredness I experienced at the time, and had kept ever since. And at long last I came to see how clearly that shadow was preventing my knowing with the mind of Christ and loving with the most Sacred Heart and that, in truth, my development was done on these two journeys until the brokenness of that devastated five year old boy was healed. I had spent all my pesos. I set out, as we all must, for that tiny, precious *matryoshka*, the lost sheep, frozen at the fulcrum of forty years before, to go after her until I found her, to lift her on my shoulders and to bring her back home.

The words on this page are quite literally not only fifteen years in the making and fifteen years in the writing; they are fifteen years in the *waiting*. For most of us, there is nothing more powerful we can do than to bring light to our darkness, healing to our shadow, and liberation to the Spirit trapped there, in order to propel our journey through states and stages—through the most Sacred Heart and the mind of Christ. From the Gospel of Thomas, listen to the words long written down: "If you bring it into being within you, that which you have will save you. If you do not have it within you, then that which you do not have within you will kill you."

In many ways I'm the last man on earth who should be writing this book. That's why I had to write it. Father Thomas reminded me with a smile, some years ago, that "you're not getting any younger!" We have a precious human birth and a precious human life with which to make love real where it counts the most, in the only place and time we'll ever have. With all your depth and presence, *be here now*. Our great colleague and friend the late James Baye used to say go beyond "bodymind dropped" to *bodymind dropped in,* and there are only so many summers, and only so many springs in which to live as love, before our embodiment is at an end.

Manna for the Journey

A beautiful friend of mine works with voice dialogue to great effect, with regard to the shadow.

Given the parable of the hundred pesos, our self-system must have one hell of a time keeping our legion of selves together! But each of them has a voice: they all have something to say. In the progression of *see it*, *talk to it*, *be it*, much of the work in reincorporating the split off parts of ourselves is to recognize those selves, be in relationship with them, understand their message to us, and welcome them home—sometimes after a lifetime of being left behind.

The practice is first to identify a part of you that's split off; you'll know it by something that triggers you, makes you angry, makes you sad. Give that voice a name so you can address it, honor it, relate with it. Then ask for permission to speak to that voice. Ask it questions: Who are you? What happened? How did that make you feel? What do you want me to know about?

Next, find in yourself a transcendent voice that corresponds to the split-off voice. For example, if the split-off voice is terrified, find the transcendent voice that is fearless in the face of that terror. Give it a name, and ask it questions too. How do you find strength to be fearless? Why is everything going to be okay? How is it that *all manner of things shall be well*?

Finally, get in touch with a third voice, at the apex of those two voices. The very fact that you can locate the first two voices within your vast self means that there is one who is witnessing those two voices, and is embracing those two selves, as her very own children. So speak to the one who knows both the terrified voice and the fearless one, and makes room for them all. And find the wisdom that she has to bring, and bring her illumination into the light of your vast self, like the Easter candle in the midst of a dark cathedral. We are like any of the Gospel stories in which, we too, are each of the characters. And we are the living book from which those characters leap into being. There is room in your heart for all things, and for each of your selves as together you become yourself. As Sufi poet Ibn Arabi has it:

O Marvel,
a garden among the flames!

My heart can take on
any form:
a meadow for gazelles,
a cloister for monks,

For the idol, sacred ground,
Ka'ba for the circling pilgrim,
the tables of the Torah,

the scrolls of the Qur'ān.

I profess the religion of love;
wherever its caravan turns along the way,
that is the belief,
the faith I keep.[3]

Why the Dark Before the Dawn?

The dark before the dawn can be heartbreaking. If your heart is broken, the Sacred Heart is broken too, and the causal heart of God. You are the one whom God has in heart, and has in mind: a mind that is ever held in God's heart. And if your heart is broken, let it be broken open; it is the home of limitless love, the meeting of heaven and earth. And it is the unstoppable force which holds the new earth without as the perfect reflection of the realized kingdom of heaven within, and closes the gap, fills in the breach and enacts the new earth in God's image and likeness, and God's love. There is a crack in everything. The light and love in your broken heart moves every being, whom you promised to come back for, in a moment outside of time.

The dark comes before the dawn so that love, which can move mountains, can move hearts, draw lines in the sand, and turn tables in this embodiment, along the way home, Jesus and Buddha as Brothers. "Faith is the bird that feels the light when the dawn is still dark," Rabindranath Tagore explained.

Youth poet laureate Amanda Gorman's inaugural poem concludes, in the most moving of closings:

> When day comes we step out of the shade,
> aflame and unafraid
> The new dawn blooms as we free it
> For there is always light,
> if only we're brave enough to see it
> If only we're brave enough to be it.[4]

You are the light of the world; a city on a hill cannot be hidden. On the lampstand, you give light to all the house—the Father's mansion with its many rooms—to all the Kosmos. Once you're aware of the majesty of the vantage point, you set out to inhabit every *state* in your most Sacred Heart. Once you're aware of the grandeur of the view, you set out to inhabit every *stage* in your Christic mind. But know as well: you can no longer bear to bear your *shadow*; we are all meant to be mothers of God. Let your light shine, first to illuminate your shadow: the beautiful parts of yourself who couldn't make the jump, because they were the poor in spirit, the least of Christ's sisters and brothers in your kingdom. And then be light from light with "the true light, which enlightens everyone, who was coming into the world."

EIGHT
BECOME HEAVEN

In an beautiful parallel to the old Christian tradition of dedicating the last verse of a hymn to the Trinity, Leonard Cohen, the gentle Jewish giant of poetry and song—in his second-hand physique—heard there was a secret chord, but he also wrote a secret verse, too: his second verse is often about Christ. In the second verse of *Suzanne*, he sings that Jesus was a sailor who had walked across the water, and I always wondered what it meant that Christ had touched our perfect body with his mind. Christ realized the kingdom of heaven; but he realized its perfect reflection, the new earth, too: the new earth which is the ground of your embodiment. Your heart is meek, and humble as his; it is literally of the earth. Your body is perfect, as all things always already are, in the mind of Christ; it is, in its perfection, touched by that mind. Now you have a choice, but if you look carefully, the choice is choice-less. Your only choice is to SHOW UP.

The Man Comes Around

In 1954, a man came around. He sang songs championing the rights of American Indians and protesting the Vietnam War. He sang for the poor, the aged, the sick, the captives. He was known as *The Man in Black*; in his song of the same title, he sings verse after verse about the poor, the hungry, the captives, the sick, the aged, modeled after the parable of the last judgement, but adapted for the America of his time.

Through half a century of recording music he began to transcend and include every musical category: he was covered by punk bands, and he himself covered Trent Reznor's "valentine to the suffering," *Hurt*, called the saddest music video of all time. Upon his death in 2003, when the tributes poured in, Bono gave the definitive one: "next to Johnny Cash, every man knows that he is a sissy."

But as attention came his way, Johnny Cash pointed beyond himself, as John the Baptist had: "there is another coming after me, and I am not worthy to untie the straps on his sandals." Jesus drew a line in the sand, and Johnny Cash walked that line. When his country music label rejected his songs honouring America's indigenous people (preferring the image of the "cowboy" who had defeated the "Indian") he recorded them himself, in defiance of his contract. His concert at Folsom Prison on January 13, 1968 was groundbreaking: it was the first live recording of a prison performance. He played many more: setting all the captives free, in their spirits if nowhere else. He came again and again to the "least of Christ's sisters and brothers" as though the movements in kindness that Jesus spoke of in the last judgement parable were his words to live by. One the last songs he wrote—"The Man Comes Around"—is a superb postmodern take on the Book of Revelation; according to Cash, his favourite album was among the last: *My Mother's Hymn Book*. The last song he wrote, Corinthians 15:55, begins "death, where is thy sting?"

Cash struggled with shadow and with addiction, but moved through states and stages—and stared down his shadow—on the way of embodied love, in his particular case. Jesus knew himself to be the Temple, knew himself the fulfillment of the scriptures, knew himself the promised of Isaiah. He went big before he went home, knowing that this world is the realm where our awesome gift of freedom can move mountains, and our incomparable gift of fullness, which is love, can change hearts.

Cash knew that the least of Christ's sisters and brothers are still among us, and he strove to take their perspective, in the mind of Christ:

> I just wanted to write a song that would tell what I thought it would be like in prison.[1]

And facing shadow, he was deeply in solidarity with everyone who must also face shadow:

> I think prison songs are popular because most of us are living in one kind of little prison or another, and whether we know it or not the words of a song about someone who is actually in a prison speak for a lot of us who might appear not to be, but really are.[2]

Cash explained, in *Man in Black*, that as long as the least of Christ's brothers and sisters remained poor, hungry, lonely, and suffering, he vowed to remain "the man in black." Up front there ought to be one, so he took matters in his own hands. And with those hands, he also points out the way of embodied love.

The Great Way and the Little Way

Not everyone is called to "go big" as Jesus Christ, Johnny Cash had done. Mother Teresa reminds us that we are called to do little things with great love. She herself took her name from St. Thérèse of Lisieux, who died at 24 in obscurity but left as her life a "little way" to God, and is now honoured as one of *only four women* "Doctors of the Catholic Church." When I spoke with eminent Buddhist teacher Daniel P. Brown, author of "Pointing out the Great Way," his eyes twinkled as he softly said "the Great Way is not far from the Little Way."

St. Francis of Assisi was praying in the ruins of an abandoned church when he heard the command "rebuild my church," at a time when the Catholic Church was rife with indulgences and corruption. He adorably understood the command to mean repair that very church; as he knelt down he put stone on top of stone with such love that Pope Urban, upon meeting him years later, dreamed that the Lateran Basilica—the most important church of Christendom, the St. Peter's of its day—was collapsing, and Francis had stepped in to take the place of the crumbled pillar.

We are called, in Mother Teresa's words, to do

"something beautiful for God." There is nothing more beautiful we could do than to empty ourselves of attachment to self, and inhabit the mind of Christ, the most Sacred Heart, and live as love, tenderly, ferociously, in our particular case. And to give our radically unique perspective to God, that God could know and love the Kosmos through our eyes, and God could move the Kosmos, with our small hands and God's limitless love, to enact the new earth, perfect reflection of the kingdom of heaven.

Brother André of Montreal was born in rural Quebec in 1845 he joined the Congregation of the Holy Cross as a brother, but was never admitted to higher studies because of his frailty: he was judged likely to die before he would be ordained. He could barely read and could hardly write, limited to simply signing his own name. He worked as the porter for Collége Notre-Dame in Cote-des-Neiges, Quebec for forty years.

But he welcomed every visitor as Christ, and people began to come to him with sadness, with brokenness, with illness. Each left him moved, with the gentlest hint of Bliss, with the lightest touch of Love. People who had arrived in illness left inexplicably in health; these were verified by the best doctors of the day, with an understanding of medicine not that different than our own. His advice echoed the injunction that Jesus gave *five times* as he bid farewell to his disciples, the night before he died: "pray, and it will happen." Though he was frail all his life, Brother André died at ninety-one years of age. As the doorman for Collége Notre-Dame, he had healed an estimated 10,000 people, not taking credit for a single one of them. Upon his canonization as a saint in 2010, Canada's national newspaper called him the "Rocket Richard" of miracles, after the prolifically scoring Montreal Canadiens' hockey player Maurice "Rocket" Richard. If something exists, it's possible.

Theosis and Theotokos

It's sublime to stand in the back of an Orthodox Church and regard the faithful as they enter for Divine Liturgy. Each makes their way up to the front and venerates the collection of icons there, depicting the heroic women and men who have walked in Christ's Way through the centuries. Upon venerating the last icon, each turns and bows to the congregation in silence, and they in silence bow back. The profound meaning of the gesture is that we too are Ikons of God, deserving of reverence, to be seen as God sees us. Raimon Panikkar echoes that we are icons of God; the task of every creature is to complete their icon. The icon of Christ in every being is Panikkar's *Christophany*. God's sanctuary is indescribably more holy, having your icon grace its walls. We are each of us a stained glass window in the chapel of sacred mirrors, shards of brokenness that are taken up in the hands of Christ and formed to make a masterpiece, in each of our cases. And the light in the chapel is infinitely more radiant for having shone through your pane, cracked though it is. I am ever grateful to Leonard Cohen, who reminds us that our very brokenness is how the light gets in.

We are even called to divinization, to *theosis*; this in fact, in Eastern Christian teachings, is very much the purpose of human life. This path comes with a singularly important instruction, a line crossed all too often through history: it is only by *catharsis* (purification of mind and body) and *theoria* (illumination with the vision of God) that theosis takes place. *Kenosis*—our emptying in surrender of the separate self-sense—is the gate to theosis. The extent of Jesus' kenosis and the depth of his eros resulted in the height of his agape: in Cynthia Borgeault's formulation, agape = eros X kenosis. "Man," said Rahner, in the gendered style of the church, and of the times, "is the mystery of infinite emptiness." And Jesus was the man. Any attempt to associate the separate self-sense with God is illusory, as Ramana began. Brahman alone is real.

In the beginning, God spoke the Word, which is Christ. Those on the way of embodied love live as an answer to the question, not "what would Jesus do?" but rather, "*what will Christ do?*" Jesus answered that question definitively, with the turning of the tables and the line in the sand. That was the life of Christ Jesus, *Christ in history*; the question now is Christ in me, Christ in you: what will *Christ in mystery* do? Christ is the divine subject and we, the predicate that completes the sentence. What are the words of love you would weave into yours? Christ is the divine subject, we the human object. But if the subject of one stage becomes the object of the subject of the next, we are to be transformed into Christ: "we will be like him, for we shall see him as he Is." Wilber reminds us that "when I am not an object, I am God. (And every I in the entire Kosmos can say that truthfully.)" Let your most Sacred Heart, your Christic mind be still and know that I Am; find rest for your souls, for Christ's yoga is easy, and Christ's burden, light. Let the body and mind of your precious human birth abide in Christ Consciousness, abide in Awareness. Thou art that.

The medieval theologian Meister Eckhart is so thoroughly nondual that many Buddhist friends of mine insist he is Buddhist! He taught that

> "We are all meant to be mothers of God. What good is it to me if this eternal birth of the divine Son takes place unceasingly, but does not take place within myself? And, what good is it to me if Mary is full of grace if I am not also full of grace? What good is it to me for the Creator to give birth to his Son if I do not also give birth to him in my time and my culture? This, then, is the fullness of time: When the Son of Man is begotten in us."[3]

Mary is given the beautiful title *Theotokos*, "who gave birth to one who was God". Meister Eckhart gives us the humbling injunction to become the same. Our love is nothing if it is not embodied. This world was created for love, or rather, love was created for this world. In each of our "original sins," it is love that forms the bridge; love, says Maharaj, "crosses the abyss." Ramana Maharshi, in his self-inquiry, instructs us to "keep the mind in the heart." Meister Eckhart also teaches:

> In this life we are to become heaven
> So that God might find a home here in us.[4]

To be clear, the Meister is calling us to an ascent *that is worthless* without a descent. God is in search of a home here, and where is God to make a home, if not here and now, the only place we will ever be, the only moment we will ever have? Jesus said "If anyone loves me, he will keep my word, and my Father will love him, and we will come to him and make our home with him." We are dust to Divinity and Divinity to dust, and more: dust-Divinity. The kingdom of heaven is in our midst (inside); the new earth is its perfect reflection (outside). Thomas gives us a perfectly non-dual injunction:

> When you make the two one and make the in-
> side like the outside and the outside like the
> inside and the above like the below, and that
> you might make the male and the female be
> one and the same. (Logion 22)

Love bridges each of the original dualities, each of the original sins. Love (the Spirit) is the bridge between being and knowing, between God Consciousness and Christ Consciousness. And thou art that. Kahlil Gibran speaks of the beauty of this Spirit: it is "rather a heart enflamed and a soul enchanted."

> People of Orphalese, beauty is life when life unveils her holy face.
> But you are life and you are the veil.
> Beauty is eternity gazing at itself in a mirror.
> But you are eternity and you are the mirror.[4]

Infinity and eternity manifest in space and in time, in you and in I, as depth (stages) and presence (states). And thou art that.

The Spirit of Evolution

The subject tonight is love. You have ended the Great Search, and reconciled original sin, which was simply to identify your body and your mind—the great vehicles of embodied love—with your self; to believe that the separate self-sense was who you were. Your body, your mind, abide in your consciousness, which is Christ's consciousness, and as your true Self, you abide in Awareness, and enter the darkest of dark nights with Christ, in the stillness and savasana of the tomb, and its radical Emptiness.

It's the early morn of the third day. The Magdalan will soon arrive with myrrh to anoint the body she believes to be dead. Now begins your Great Duty, your Great Dharma, the resurrection in your case, which means nothing unless it means everything in you, and in me. You consciously choose your manifestation, and you choose yourself (Oscar Wilde reminds you that "everyone else is taken."). But you choose yourself as you're known in the mind of Christ, as you're loved in the most Sacred Heart. In your heart and nowhere else, "the kingdom is in the midst." Your Great Duty is the enaction of "on earth as it is in heaven." You are dust, and to dust you will return. But in your precious, sacred heart is the Temple, the Holy of Holies, and Divinity is tabernacled there; you are Divinity too, in the *kenosis* of your humanity. So you are dust-Divinity, and you've promised to remind all beings that they are dust-Divinity too. Awareness in you has awakened. In *jnana drishti*, that awakened Awareness in you knows and loves Awareness, still slumbering, in all beings.

A mystery among mysteries is how we could possibly "do greater things than these, since I am going to the Father": to heal the sick, give sight to the blind. To speak heartbreakingly beautiful words of love to the heartbroken. To draw lines in the sand fearlessly; to overturn tables with ferocity. To raise the dead, including his own broken body.

In evolution, we have the answer. Jesus' "return to the Father" completes the Alpha to the Omega, the involutionary jump, and the evolutionary return. The canvas of our evolutionary future is imbued with the signature love of Christ; the new stages emerging are ours to fill in—greater stages than were there in the days of Jesus—and that canvas awaits us, and the breathtaking valley beyond, the view seen in clarity from our vantage point. The sacred brush is in our hands. The love of God attracts the love of Christ in all sentient beings and draws all beings to God's self in love. Eternity, it is true, is in love with the productions of time. Heaven and earth are united in this most Sacred Heart that beats within your breast; the consciousness of Christ empowers you to see Christ as consciousness in all sentient beings, and there to know Christ and to love Christ. To move in the world with the freedom of a nondual realization in your awakened, most Sacred Heart, and the fullness of *metanoia*, the supermind of Christ. And raise the poor up from the dust, even as we too are Cohen's troubled dust; we too are Cohen's solitude of longing. And with this meek, humble human heart—after Jesus' heart—to heal the broken Heart above.

Our task is to come into the kingdom of heaven, in the eternal *now*. And to enact "on earth as it is in heaven" in our consciousness, in our case: through our minds, in our bodies, but imbued with the mind of Christ, and with Christ's most Sacred Heart. "Of the future, your task is not to predict it, but to enable it," as Antoine de St-Exupery put it.

The Spirit of evolution—subtitle to *Sex, Ecology, Spirituality*—is the Spirit Christ sends to us, and what draws us back to God, with the same momentum with which Spirit dove into us, as us, in the first place. Spirit pours into evolution in a particular, incomparably unique way in the Supermind of the latest stage, the nondual state, to which all are invited. There "the forms are descending, unadulterated." And greater still: in Cynthia Borgeault's formulation, Agape = Eros X Kenosis; the power of Agape that emanates from us is equal to the power of Eros that moves through us times the emptiness that we cultivate, to be the mirror which reflects the Spirit back to its Source.

Cynthia, *I see your formulation and I raise you*: Agape = Eros^{Kenosis} [A = E^{K}]: the Agape that emanates is our Eros *to the power of* Kenosis, our emptying. We know that power from the life of Jesus; it is Christ the Omega who is Always Already here, now to show the fullness of that power in the infinity of the emptiness that we offer.

The mind of Christ is vast—vaster than in Jesus' day, with twenty centuries of human thought, human growth, human love. And Christ the Omega calls us from closer by, in the kingdom of heaven, in the midst of the new earth. We are to do greater things than these, in the Spirit of evolution. As spoke Saul Williams: "God's just a baby. And her diaper is wet."

𝔚ith the 𝔖pirit, and 𝔚ith 𝔉ire

In my end is my beginning.

We began our journey on *The Way of Embodied Love* with the words of John the Forerunner:

> "I baptize you with water. But one who is more powerful than I will come, the straps of whose sandals I am not worthy to untie. He will baptize you with the Holy Spirit and fire." (Luke 3:16)

What is the baptism with the Holy Spirit, the baptism with fire?

From Awareness springs consciousness as *Satchitananda*: Being, Knowing and Loving. From God as *Being* (I Am who Am) we take form: an idea of priceless beauty and sacred love in the divine mind: the Word, the *Knowing* of God. That Word is spoken through the *Loving* Spirit, through which Divinity becomes dust: The Word becomes flesh. That flesh is a temple of Christ Consciousness, with the mind of Christ and the most Sacred Heart. And thou art that.

To be baptized in the Spirit is to receive the gift of being, in this precious human birth, with the mind of Christ and the most Sacred Heart. The Spirit is the Spirit of evolution, and the Spirit draws us back to herself and to Christ the Omega, precisely as evolution. One was tabernacled among us—the Bodhisattva of Love, the nondual Master of the West—and revealed to us "on earth as it is in Heaven," even as the Bodhisattva of Compassion, the nondual Master of the East realized: "emptiness is none other than form; form is none other than emptiness." The Koran has it: "God's is the East, and God's is the West. Therefore look to the East or look to the West, and there you shall behold the face of God." It was always so, but Christ as Jesus revealed to us what is Always Already the Way, the Truth, the Life.

> *Let the same mind be in you that was in Christ Jesus,*
> who, though he was in the form of God,
> did not regard equality with God
> as something to be exploited,
> but emptied himself,
> taking the form of a slave,
> being born in human likeness.
> And being found in human form,
> he humbled himself
> and became obedient to the point of death—
> even death on a cross.
> Therefore God also highly exalted him
> and gave him the name
> that is above every name. (Philippians 2:5-9)

At the name of Jesus ("I Am who Am, and it is I that rescues.") we know the way: let our consciousness, held and beheld by the mind of Christ and Christ's most Sacred Heart, abide in Awareness, and there find rest, there practice *yoga,* union with the Divine.

And then spring into action in this world; let the Divinity so animate the dust with love that we have the courage to draw the lines in the sand that must be drawn, and turn the tables that must be turned, in this day and age. The writing on the wall is in your hand. There can be no doubt that we are being baptized by fire: *our world is burning*. We are faced with truly wicked problems—racism, climate, poverty, technology, demagoguery. Humanity's predicament, in its isolation, its desolation, is bad.

We are faced with hyperobjects—in the words of Einstein, prescient today on every front:

> Our world faces a crisis as yet unperceived by those possessing power to make great decisions for good or evil. The unleashed power of the atom has changed everything save our modes of thinking and we thus drift toward unparalleled catastrophe. We scientists who released this immense power have an overwhelming responsibility in this world life-and-death struggle to harness the atom for the benefit of mankind and not for humanity's destruction. We need two hundred thousand dollars at once for a nation-wide campaign to let people know that *a new type of thinking is essential if mankind is to survive and move toward higher levels.*[5]

How else to prehend the many hyperobjects we face, but with the mind of Christ (by any other name)? How else to solve the wicked problems but with the most Sacred Heart of love—now gentle, now ferocious, as the novel emergent?

The least of Christ's sisters and brothers—and therefore Christ—are imprisoned in China, are butchered in Myanmar, are dying in India, are slaughtered in Yemen. Evil shows its face at the Capitol riot. We are in a global pandemic, like the leprosy in Jesus' day. Christ cries on the cross "I am thirsty"; Christ cries on a street in Minneapolis "I can't breathe, man." Our tonglen, our exchange of self and other, breathes infinite compassion with the breath after George Floyd breathed his last: the breath he could never take. We are called to practice that tonglen at the foot of the cross, with Mary of Magdala, with Mary his mother, with the disciple whom Jesus loved. And we exchange self and other in the most Sacred Heart—the heart of Christ, where heaven meets earth—that also beats within our breast. And who is "the disciple whom Jesus loved?" Thou art that.

ARRIVAL

We saw that one emerged from the stable at Bethlehem—Jesus our brother—and that he emerged from the waters of the Jordan under John the Forerunner's baptism, and that he emerged from the radically empty tomb of Golgatha, having extended his wakefulness beyond waking, beyond dreaming, beyond deep sleep and by all accounts—though without explanation—beyond death. We saw that he knew and loved the Torah and the Temple, and treasured God's promise to return to Israel. We saw that he had plenty of reflections on the turning away, and he ever moved to be radically emptied—his equality with God not something to be "exploited"—so that love could find a home here, in his sacred human heart. He took the highest vantage point that his state of consciousness could offer, and he beheld the widest view that his stage of consciousness could interpret from, with his entire being in light, having liberated the captive selves in shadow.

What this meant was, in the nondual master-piece, *becoming* I Am who Am, *becoming* the great Thou in the I-Thou relationship with the least of his sisters, brothers, who are all beings, *becoming* body and blood in the mystery of the water and the wine, so that everyone could touch him, taste him, *become* him in their case: "all Buddhas throughout space and time." He lived perfectly "on earth as it is in heaven" and equally, "emptiness is not other than form, and form is not other than emptiness." He did these things and from the threshold of whatever realization he had attained, he *came back*, into the heart of infinite suffering, bringing that suffering into his own heart of limitless love. The Pharisees summoned up a thunder-cloud; they heard from him, and we have definitively heard from Jesus.

We know that Jesus went to "prepare a place for us." The writer of the incomparably profound Gospel of John was traditionally assumed to be "the disciple whom Jesus loved" but we now know that he was not; the writer of the Gospel intended that disciple to be you, to be me. It was you, the disciple beloved of Jesus, who rested your head on Jesus' Sacred Heart, asking with infinite tenderness and untold sadness, "who is it who will betray you, Lord?" It was I, the disciple beloved of Jesus, who remained at the foot of his cross, with Mary his mother and Mary of Magdala, our names—as Isaiah 49 tells us—carved on the palms of his hands. Because he had the courage to never turn away from us, we too take the courage to never turn away from him. We can answer, to the hauntingly beautiful old spiritual *Were You There?* Yes, we were there.

But Saint Paul reveals the mystery even further:

> To them God has chosen to make known among the Gentiles the glorious riches of this mystery, which is Christ in you, the hope of glory. (Colossians 1:27)

Christ in Mystery is Christ in you! You have the honour beyond imagination of a precious human birth, and a precious human life. Alongside your beautifully beating gross heart and your inexpressibly precious subtle heart beats the causal, most Sacred Heart of Christ. Meta to your mind, in *metanoia*, is the Mind of Christ, yours to wear like a starry crown. With Christ's heart and Christ's mind, you take up

Christ's *yoga*—union with God—which is effortless, and you find rest for your soul, which becomes still and knows that "I Am God." Your true Self, who is Christ, beholds God with the same eye with which God beholds that Self, and you become mother of God, for you have become heaven so that God could find a home here. Your true Self abides in Awareness, and you slip into the nondual masterpiece.

You are dust to Divinity and Divinity to dust; you are dust-Divinity. Like Manjushri, you say "let the one who has not sinned," and you draw the line in the sand. And you will never turn away, never hesitate to love with the ferocity that turns tables, ever move to love with the tenderness that lifts the woman "caught in adultery" from the dust, because you've silenced her accusers, and neither do you condemn her.

Be transformed in *metanoia*, with the mind of Christ, and Christ's most Sacred Heart. Know God in your Christic heart—God who dances as *Lila* in all of creation, who dances you to the end of Love in the secret room, and as whom you dance, "I Am who Am"—through the great states of consciousness. See all things as Christ sees them in your Christic mind, through the great stages of consciousness. Bring light to the little matryoshkas, the split off selves left behind in shadow, alone and afraid all these years; let their voices be heard, their teachings received, their love reunited. Then abide in Awareness. And as Awakened, act decisively.

Christ is your true Self, adorned like a lily of the field with the beauty of you, unique in all the Kosmos. The evangelist John—who saw heaven and earth pass away, and "the new heaven" within and "the new earth" without—saw too that "we shall be like Christ, for we shall see Christ as Christ is." The kingdom of heaven has come very close to you; the humble shall inherit the earth. And thou art that.

Epilogue

There is an Other
Become the Other
There is no Other

—Father Bede Griffiths,
to a monk of Snowmass, in a dream

"...was looking at the crucifix
got something in my eye,
a light that doesn't need to live
and doesn't need to die.

A riddle in the Book of Love
obscure and obsolete
till witnessed here in time and blood
a thousand kisses deep."

—Leonard Cohen spoken in concert,
Vancouver, B.C., Canada,
December 2, 2010

Bibliography

Departure

1. Kant, Immanuel, *Akademie Ausgabe, Groundwork of the Metaphysics of Morals* (1785), 4:421.

Chapter 1

1. Merton, Thomas, *New Seeds of Contemplation* (New York: New Directions, 1961), 30.

2. Eckhart, Meister, *Sermons, Writings and Sayings* (London: New Seeds: 2005), xi.

3. Gibran, Kahlil *The Prophet* (New York: Knopf, 1923), 16.

Chapter 2

1. Eckhart, Meister, *Sermons, Writings and Sayings* (London: New Seeds: 2005), xi.

2. Sri Nisargadatta Maharaj, *I Am That* (Bombay: maharajnisgaradatta.com, 1981), 160.

3. Sri Nisargadatta Maharaj, *I Am That* (Bombay: maharajnisgaradatta.com, 1981), 204.

4. Wilber, Ken, *The Religion of Tomorrow* (Boulder: Shambhala, 2017), 214.

5. Wilber, Ken, *The Religion of Tomorrow* (Boulder: Shambhala, 2017), 215.

6. Wilber, Ken, *The Religion of Tomorrow* (Boulder: Shambhala, 2017), 222.

7. Wilber, Ken, *The Religion of Tomorrow* (Boulder: Shambhala, 2017), 226.

8. Wilber, Ken, *The Religion of Tomorrow* (Boulder: Shambhala, 2017), 227.

9. Gibran, Kahlil, *Jesus the Son of Man* (New York: Knopf, 1928), 105.

Chapter 3

1. Gibran, Kahlil, *Jesus the Son of Man* (New York: Knopf, 1928), 51.

2. Gibran, Kahlil, *The Prophet* (New York: Knopf, 1923), 102.

3. Sri Nisargadatta Maharaj, *I Am That* (Bombay: maharajnisgaradatta.com, 1981), 13.

4. Sri Nisargadatta Maharaj, *I Am That* (Bombay: maharajnisgaradatta.com, 1981), 13.

Chapter 4

1. Gibran, Kahlil, *The Prophet* (New York: Knopf, 1923), 66.

2. Wilber, Ken, *The Religion of Tomorrow* (Boulder: Shambhala, 2017), 394.

3. de Saint-Exupéry, Antoine *The Wisdom of the Sands* (Paris: Gallimard, 1948), 152.

Chapter 5

1. Gibran, Kahlil, *Jesus the Son of Man* (New York: Knopf, 1928), 109.

2. Merton, Thomas, *New Seeds of Contemplation* (New York: New Directions, 1961), 4.

3. Cantor, Rachel, *Good on Paper* (Brooklyn: Melville House, 2016), 211.

4. Carlson, Rebecca, in a poem to Ken Wilber.

5. Wilber, Ken, *One Taste* (Boulder: Shambhala, 200), 151.

6. Merton, Thomas, *New Seeds of Contemplation* (New York: New Directions, 1961), 45.

Chapter 6

1. Straughn, Harold Kent, "Stages of Faith: an Interview with James Fowler" *John Mark Ministries*, 13 Oct 2006, jmm.org.au/articles/18316. Accessed 9 May 2021.

2. Kant, Immanuel, *Akademie Ausgabe, Groundwork of the Metaphysics of Morals* (1785), 4:421.

3. Wilber, Ken, *Integral Semiotics: The Language of Liberation* (Boulder: Integral Life, 2017), 18.

Chapter 7

1. Tolkien, J. R.R., *The Return of the King: The Lord of th Rings Part 3* (London: Allen & Unwin, 1955 , 1044.

2. Muhyiddin Ibn Arabi , *Tarjuman al-ashwaq Poem 11* c. 1200).

3. Gorman, Amanda, *The Hill We Climb: An Inaugural Poem for the Country* (New York: Viking, 2021).

Chapter 8

1. Streissguth, Michael, *Johnny Cash at Folsom Prison: The Making of a Masterpiece* (Boston: De Capo Press, 2005).

2. Horstman, Dorothy, *Sing Your Heart Out, Country Boy* (New York: Pocket Books, 1976), 292.

3. Von Balthasar, Hans Urs, *Love Alone is Credible* (San Fransicso: Ignatius Press, 2005), 42.

4. Edwards, Gill, *Wild Love: Discover the Magical Secrets of Freedom, Joy and Unconditional Love* (London: Little, Brown Book Group, 2006).

5. Gibran, Kahlil, *The Prophet* (New York: Knopf, 1923), 85.

6. (25 May 1946) "Atomic Education Urged by Einstein" *New York Times,* 11.

Acknowledgments

I'm deeply grateful to a small sangha for their massive contributions toward helping this book, a long time in coming, manifest at long last. Dustin DiPerna and Brad Reynolds moved mountains to allow a manuscript that was written over Holy Week to be published by Pentecost, with their man-to-man challenges and their lifting me up as though I was not heavy; as though I was their brother. This book is written as a book of love—in a long lineage of books of love—and you'll find the art of Dust-in Divinity and Sri B. on every page. I'm profoundly grateful to the Integral Community for their Awakened Love, especially Gail Hochachka, Colin Bigelow, Angie Hinickle, Jeff Salzman, Marco Morelli, Corey deVos, David Riordan, Jennifer Walton, Robert Richards and Ellen Braun. A deep bow to Rob McNamara, my brother who has met me—week in and week out—for a decade, at a location that God only knows. Namaste to Nomali Perera, who spoke with the compassion of Avalokiteshvara to the little matryoshka who'd split off into shadow, in my case. And I'm ever grateful to my teachers: Ken Wilber, who has as big a mind as you'll find, but also a heart to match; and Father Thomas Keating, ever-present in the retinue who lift our steps along the way of embodied love.

Roland Michael Stanich is a lifelong Catholic contemplative based in Canada. As a long term student of both Father Thomas Keating and Ken Wilber, Stanich brings a modern synthesis to the Christian Tradition informed by developmental psychology and an in-depth knowledge of other religious and spiritual traditions. He served as Chief Facilitator for Integral Spiritual Center, an initiative of twenty prominent spiritual teachers from more than a dozen spiritual traditions, all gathered to explore the significance and impact of Ken Wilber's Integral theory on their own lineages. Stanich was also chosen by Father Thomas Keating to represent Christianity at the groundbreaking Snowmass Interspiritual Dialogues. He currently works with a startup company researching plasma physics for abundant, clean energy, and is building Metamind, an Artificial Intelligence application designed to enable human[AI].

CPSIA information can be obtained
at www.ICGtesting.com
Printed in the USA
LVHW072322200821
695736LV00010B/267